Through the Darkness, into the Light

Ellen Cheryl

WESTBOW
PRESS®
A DIVISION OF THOMAS NELSON
& ZONDERVAN

WestBow Press books may be ordered through booksellers or by contacting:

WestBow Press
A Division of Thomas Nelson & Zondervan
1663 Liberty Drive
Bloomington, IN 47403
www.westbowpress.com
1 (866) 928-1240

Interior Image Credit: Sarah Adams

ISBN: 978-1-9736-7982-0 (sc)
ISBN: 978-1-9736-7983-7 (hc)
ISBN: 978-1-9736-7981-3 (e)

Library of Congress Control Number: 2019918618

Print information available on the last page.

WestBow Press rev. date: 11/20/2019

Dedication

To our Lord and Savior, and to my brothers and sisters, whom I love with all my heart and soul.

Acknowledgment

To my friends, for their hard work, support, and dedication
to this project, and their artistic talent. Thank you.

Contents

Contents

Do I Truly Forgive and Understand?

When I see the faults of others
am I grateful I'm not there?
If I am, I'm false to myself,
for what I don't like of you,
I don't like of me,
and I'm afraid to see.
I have no understanding of them
because I have no understanding of me.
When I see how empty I was
and how I hated me
when I gave up on life,
I gave up on me,
but when I walk in their shoes
and feel and see,
then I truly forgive and understand.
I forgave me.

Chapter 1
The Early Years

I was born in February 1944. Dad had left two months before I was born. He went to the South Pacific to fight in the Second World War. How fearful those times must have been for Mom and Dad, not knowing if he would be coming back, if they would see each other again, or when Dad would see me for the first time or get to see my older sister, Sarah, and John, my brother, again.

In the spring of 1944, Dad, living in fear and uncertainty for his life, sent three Easter cards from the Philippines, one for each of his children. This was my first Easter. The cards were all identical, with a mama duck and three baby ducks on the cover. He wrote on the inside of my card,

> To my darling daughter, Ellen, whom I may never
> see. May you grow up to be as wonderful and lovely
> as your mother!
>
> Love,
> Daddy

I still hold the significance of my card dearly in my heart. Of course, Mom kept them for us.

Being grateful and blessed, Mom and Dad did see each other again, with Dad coming home after the war ended. How exciting and wonderful it must have been when he came home. Mom became pregnant right away with my younger brother, Hank. Sara was five, John was four, and I was almost two years old. Now there were four of us kids.

With all the men and women coming home from the war, there was a housing shortage. My parents needed to find another home because the landlord of the house they rented during the war needed it for himself and his family.

Dad found a house. The house was condemned, as it was not up to code. It was owned by the city for back taxes. He was able to buy it from the city.

When we moved there, I was three. The house was small. It had one bedroom on the main floor. The living room was about twelve feet by fourteen feet, and there was a small kitchen with a pump and no running water—just the pump—at the kitchen sink. No bathroom. There was an outhouse.

Dad and Grandpa put a new roof on the house first because it leaked. Dad installed a new furnace, taking up a quarter of the living room. It could burn wood or coal. This house didn't have a basement.

I remember Mom heating water on the stove in the kitchen. There was a shed off the kitchen with a large tub where we would take our baths—first Mom and Dad and then us kids. Later, Dad would build a bathroom off their bedroom with a toilet and shower, with hot and cold water throughout the house. It was wonderful.

Sara, John, and I slept in the attic. Hank slept in a crib in Mom and Dad's bedroom.

Life was at a much slower pace than it is today. This was a time of change. Still, some things were of the past.

We had an icebox, not a refrigerator. The iceman would deliver ice every other day. When he would pull up in his truck, every kid on the street would run up to him begging for a small piece of ice. I remember the large leather patch on his shoulder and the huge metal tongs he used to pick up the big piece of ice. He would put the ice on his shoulder to carry it into the house. It was my job to remind Mom to empty the pan of water at the bottom of the icebox so the water wouldn't overflow onto the floor.

A dairy company delivered milk on our street. His cart was pulled by horses. All the kids used to love petting them. Sometimes, we would feed them a carrot or an apple.

A local bakery delivered freshly baked goods every day. It also had horses pulling a cart.

There were no supermarkets, just a local grocery store, where we bought fresh meat and vegetables every day because we had an icebox. Flour and sugar were in barrels. They were weighed and bought by the pound. Pickles were in barrels also. Ice cream was a rare treat. Mom would buy just enough for each of us to have a small bowl.

Dad taught me how to swim before I was three years old. There was a city park just a few blocks from our house with a huge pool. Swimming was free at all city pools.

When Sara was seven and I was three, we went to the park. When we checked in to go swimming, the guard said I was too small. The shallow part of the pool was three feet deep. The water would be over my head.

Sara and I told the guard I knew how to swim. She didn't believe us and said I could go to the wading pool for little kids. I was crying. I wanted to go swimming in the big pool.

Sara found a friend to go swimming with. You needed to have a buddy to swim.

I was crying and disappointed as I walked all the way back home alone. I told Mom they wouldn't let me swim. I was too little.

Mom comforted me, telling me that everything would be okay. She took me by my hand, and we walked back to the park.

Mom asked to see the park director, Mr. Socks. She told him I knew how to swim, that Dad had taught me. All Mom wanted was an opportunity for me to prove I could swim. She would take full responsibility for me.

3

After some time, Mr. Socks relented. He said to bring me to the pool the next morning at eight o'clock. If I could swim across the deep end of the pool and back, I would be allowed to swim.

The next morning, I was so excited. When Mom and I arrived at the pool, Mr. Socks and a pool guard were standing next to the pool.

I walked up to the pool. Mr. Socks thought I was going to jump in at the side of the pool. But I climbed up to the diving board. I was showing off. He wanted me to get down, but Mom reassured him that I would be okay. Dad had taught me how to dive as well. I dove in.

The length of the pool was one hundred feet. I swam freestyle. When I got to the other end, I turned and dove under the water. I swam all the way back to the other end of the pool underwater. I was like a little tadpole.

Mr. Socks and the pool guard were astonished. I was allowed to swim at the big pool. I went swimming every day, all summer long.

That same summer, Sara snuck a candle and matches up to the attic. We had all been taught the dangers of playing with fire, especially with Dad being a fireman. He was working that day.

While Mom was making dinner, and John and I were playing outside, Sara was upstairs playing with the matches. She lit the candle.

Later, Mom called all of us to dinner. Sara left the candle burning. While we were eating, we smelled smoke. Mom noticed the smoke coming from the stairs to the attic. She tried to go upstairs, but the smoke was too thick. She immediately called the fire department.

Within minutes, the fire department arrived. The firemen went upstairs, including Dad. It was his fire station that got the fire alarm. While the firemen were putting out the fire, Mom ordered all three of us—Sara, John, and me—to sit on the sofa in the living room. Hank was too small. She suspected it was one of us who had started the fire.

After the fire was out, Dad came into the living room, blackened from the smoke and with sweat running down his face. His eyes were ablaze with anger as he glared at all three of us. If looks could kill, all three of us would be dead. I had never seen him so angry. We were terrified.

John and I blurted out, "We didn't do it, Daddy."

Sara was silent.

Mom interjected, "I'll tell you who started the fire when you come home tomorrow morning." She had already figured out who the guilty party was.

I can imagine how embarrassing this was for Dad, being the lieutenant at the fire station and in charge of the men. One of his kids started a fire at his own house.

It was good Dad had the night to calm down. Sara got a spanking the next morning and couldn't go out to play for a couple of days. I was glad it wasn't me.

We had a radio for entertainment. It was three feet tall and about two feet wide.

The next-door neighbors were the first to get a television. Mom, my siblings, and I were asked to come over to see it. The TV was as big as our radio, but the screen was about three inches round. It had a big magnifying glass over the screen to make the picture look bigger.

I almost got into trouble. I was about to say, "Big deal," when Mom elbowed me. She knew what I was about to say. I shut up. I was about six or seven years old.

We didn't have a car. Dad had a racing bike that he rode back and forth to work. Being a fireman for the city, he was home every other Sunday. We would walk to church, which was about a mile from our house. It was difficult for Mom to take the four of us when Dad wasn't home.

Church was very important with our family. We learned about our Father in heaven and his Son, Christ, who was born on Christmas to save us all from our sins.

I would go to Sunday school. Mom would always give me a quarter to put in the collection plate. I was five or six years old at the time. One Sunday, I kept the quarter. On Monday, I walked to the five and ten cent store. I bought a baby bottle for my doll with the quarter. Mom saw me playing with my doll and the baby bottle, and she asked me where I got the bottle. I told her the store gave it to me because the bottle had a hole in the bottom and the store couldn't sell it. Mom looked at the bottom of the bottle. "There's no hole in the bottom. How did you get this?"

I wouldn't answer her. She sent me to my room in the attic. She said I could come down only when I would tell her the truth about how I got the bottle.

Being in the attic alone felt like an eternity. I agonized over what story I could come up with that my mom would believe. She always knew when I was lying. Moms are like that. Having this unseen instinct, I finally went downstairs, scared and crying. I told Mom that I kept the quarter from Sunday school and bought the baby bottle with the money.

I expected to get a spanking. Instead, Mom took me back to the five and dime and asked for the manager. She told me I needed to tell the manager I had kept the money from Sunday school and used it to buy the baby bottle, and that I needed to return it. Which I did, crying all the while. I was so ashamed. I thought my punishment was over.

Instead, the next Sunday, when we went to church, Mom went with me to Sunday school. She told me I needed to tell my teacher I stole the money and then give the money to her. Telling my Sunday school teacher was terrifying and painful. I was so ashamed and crying. I needed to admit lying and stealing three times: to Mom, the store manager, and my Sunday school teacher. That punishment was more painful than getting a spanking.

One Christmas Eve, when I was about five or six years old, I was excited about Santa Claus coming. Dad was working, and Mom had sent us to bed.

We had a dormer in the attic with a window seat. I was sitting there, looking out the window. John asked what I was doing.

I said, "I'm waiting to see Santa come."

He laughed and said, "There is no Santa Claus; Mom and Dad are Santa."

I started crying. "That's not true," I said. "You're lying."

I ran downstairs. I was still crying and told Mom what John had said. She told me the truth: There was a Santa Claus who lived a long time ago, who gave gifts to children. Parents carry on his tradition of giving gifts. I guess I was okay with what she said; I don't remember.

Christmas was very special. Going to church to celebrate the birth of Christ, being together, the radio playing Christmas carols. We would all sing along. Our Christmas tree was artificial with silk needles. It was about four feet tall, sitting on top of the radio because the living room was so small. Some of the ornaments were from Mom's Christmas tree when she was young. When we were older and leaving home, Mom gave each of us some of the old ornaments. I still have one.

We didn't get a lot of toys or presents. There wasn't a lot of money. We would get one toy. Mom would make us a pair of pajamas each. Something in clothes for church or school. We would always get a plate each with homemade cookies, some fruit, and nuts.

I remember one Christmas, Mom made us each a teddy bear out of brown corduroy material. She used buttons for the eyes and nose. To make each bear different, she used different colored yarn on each one. With the yarn, she blanket-stitched around the ears and paws. I loved my teddy bear and kept it for years.

Dad built a dogsled, and he drove it with all of us kids tucked into a blanket on the sled. Rex, our dog, would pull all of us. Rex was huge, part husky and part timber wolf (there wasn't a law at the time prohibiting owning a dog that was part wolf). He weighed about 140 pounds. He was born for this, and he loved it. Rex was loving and gentle with all of us.

Dad, weighing 175 pounds, was six feet, one inch tall. Him combined with the weight of all of us kids must have been heavy. Dad would yell, "Mush," and Rex would take off running up the street toward the open field at the end of the road, the bells on his harness jingling. Riding through the snow in the open field, all of us singing "Jingle Bells." Christmas was about sharing the joy of being together, laughing, and singing. The focus wasn't on presents, as it is today. Those are my happiest and fondest memories of Christmas of my young childhood.

Dad got a car in 1949. It was about ten or twelve years old. He got it for doing a plumbing job. He would do side jobs on his days off from being a fireman.

In January of 1952, we had heavy snowstorms. I was seven years old. I wanted to go out to play. It would take me five minutes or more to get dressed to go outside, putting on extra heavy socks, pants, snow pants, a shirt, sweater, jacket, scarf, hat, boots, and mittens. With all of the layers of clothing, I could barely move. I felt like a stuffed sausage. Mom insisted we wear all of this heavy garb to keep warm.

The snow was above my waist in the yard. Trying to make a snowman was next to impossible, so we built a snow fort instead, tunneling through the snow and packing it to make the walls.

Mom took a picture of me, standing on a snowbank made from front-end loaders because there was so much snow. Snowplows couldn't clear the road. The snowbank was so high, you could just see the roof of the grocery store on the corner with me standing on top.

We couldn't go sliding down the hills with the snow being so deep, so we went sliding on a hill in the road. Our street had very little traffic. The older kids would watch and let us know when it was all clear to go. Of course, it was dangerous. Some parents came out and yelled for us to stop, so we did. I am glad Mom and Dad didn't know. I would have gotten a spanking. I will always remember that winter.

Chapter 2
Questioning and Changing Belief

In the spring of 1952, we moved to a newer house that was only two years old. Wow, what a change. There was a large living room, two bedrooms, a bathroom with a bathtub and shower, and the kitchen, all on the main floor. There was an upstairs, and a full basement with a gas furnace. We also had a refrigerator with a freezer.

When I was eight or nine years old, we got a television with a twelve-inch screen. Of course, it was black-and-white (colored TVs had not been invented yet; they came out in 1954). I remember when Dad turned it on. The first picture was an airplane flying. This was a big deal. There were only two channels: channel 8 and 3; channel 13 came a few years later, better known as NBC, CBS, and ABC. TV was free then.

Sara and I shared a bedroom on the main floor. John and Hank had the upstairs. Dad built a rec room with a built-in gas grill in the basement. At the other end of the room, he installed two aquariums into the wall, thirty gallons each.

Back in the 1940s and early 1950s, everyone with a phone had what was called a party line. Five or six different homes would share a phone line. We would have to wait for the other person to get off the line in order to use the phone. Sometimes, us kids would listen in on the other person's conversations, until we were caught.

Just like the street we lived on before, as well as this street we moved to, there were no girls my age for me to play with. Being born between my two brothers, I played with my brothers and all the boys on our street. I was a tomboy. We spent our time climbing trees, building tree houses, playing pirates, and catching frogs, minnows, and tadpoles.

One day, Dad asked me and John to catch crickets for him for fishing. John and I walked down to the end of our street, where there was a field and woods.

We had already caught a lot of crickets, but we were still looking to catch more. John turned over a large rock, and under it was a big snake. It was coiled up, hissing and striking at us. John and I ran, leaving the cricket cage by the snake. John wanted me to get the cricket cage.

I said, "No, you go get it."

He answered, "No, you go get it."

The snake was still there, coiled up and ready to strike. Then John told me to kill the snake. We argued back and forth, who was going to kill the snake and get the cricket cage. We would have been in trouble if we left it. The snake never moved; we were hoping it would slither away. I finally relented. I picked up a big rock, went back, and killed it and got the cricket cage. My big brave brother, who was supposed to protect me, had me go kill that nasty snake, never thinking his little sister could have been bitten.

The snake was dead, with its head crushed. The body and tail were still moving. I told John he could pick it up with a stick. We wanted to take it home. Both of us were wondering why it was still moving, being dead. The snake was about two and a half feet long. John carried the snake with two sticks, with his arms straight out in front of him.

When we got home, we showed Mom the snake. We asked her why it was still moving, being dead. She said it was just the nerves still moving. It would stop moving at sundown, and it did. What sundown had to do with it, I didn't understand.

Sara was afraid of everything: frogs, snakes, turtles, bugs, and spiders, typical for a girl of that time. One day, Hank and I put a rubber spider on her pillow, on her bed. The spider was about half an inch long. It looked real. We waited for her to go into the bedroom. When she walked into the bedroom, of course, Hank and I were watching. Sara screamed bloody murder and ran out of the room. Hank and I were rolling on the floor, laughing. Sara was yelling for someone to go kill the spider. We were laughing even harder. Hank went into the bedroom and got the spider. He walked up to Sara, backed into a corner, and stuck it in her face. She was screaming and trembling all over.

She yelled, "Get that thing away from me."

Hank and I were laughing, telling her that it was only rubber, not real.

She screamed at us, "I don't care; get it away from me."

When she realized we were telling the truth, she ran after us. Hank and I ran outside, got on our bikes, and rode away. When we came home later, Sarah was still angry but left us alone. Mom had come home. Of course, we always pulled these pranks when Mom and Dad were not there.

Hank loved to scare all the girls. He caught a baby garter snake, about four inches long. He put the snake in his mouth, walked up to the girls, and let the snake crawl out of his mouth. The girls screamed and ran away. He pulled the snake out of his mouth, laughing. The next time he tried the same trick, the snake started crawling down his throat, and Hank was gagging. He stuck his hand in his mouth, pulled the snake out by its tail, and threw it on the ground. He never tried to pull that stunt again.

Another time, Hank came home with a big rusty can. The lid was still partially attached. He was holding the lid down to keep what he caught from getting out.

He came into the living room, holding the can lid down with a bloody hand, and said, "He bit me, but I finally caught him."

John lifted the lid just a little and peeked inside. He said, "It's a rat."

Mom yelled, "Get that thing out of here."

John took it outside. Hank went to the hospital. He was the most daring kid I ever knew.

Another time, Hank and I took a gallon dried-out paint can and filled it with dried grass, weeds, and sticks. I go a ring of baloney. We climbed up to the tree house, which was just a platform. We had a fire going in the paint can with the baloney stuck on sticks, and we cooked it over the fire. Dad saw us and yelled for us to put the fire out and get down from the tree. We had a bottle of water with us and immediately put out the fire.

When we got down from the tree, both of us got out bottoms warmed with a spanking. He let us know how dangerous it was having fire in the paint can. The paint can could have exploded because of the chemicals in the dried paint, and we could have been seriously hurt or possibly killed, not to mention the probability of setting the tree on fire.

I played marbles all the time with the boys. I was really good, winning almost all the time. I wrestled and fought with them as well. Many a time, I would come home from school with my dress torn, the sleeve or sash ripped. I would always say, "So-and-so did it," naming the boy. Mom got to the point where she couldn't repair them anymore.

One time during recess, I was playing marbles. Danny was really handsome, and all the girls liked him, except me. I didn't; he was so conceited. I was playing with him and won all his marbles. He was angry and started hitting me. I ran into school, all the way to my classroom, with him chasing me. Danny was taller than I was. I was fighting back and losing. He pushed me down with my back on top of a desk. Some boys went out and told the teacher what was happening, and she ran into the room, pulling Danny off me. He was sent to the principal's office. The guys told the teacher that I had won all his marbles, fair and square. Danny was angry losing to a girl, and of course, my dress was ripped again.

When I was ten years old, my brothers and I were playing in the backyard. We were swinging on the clothes pole. I was too short to reach the bar, so John lifted me up so I could grab the bar and swing. Swinging back and forth, I misjudged when to let go in order to land on my feet. Swinging out too far, I let go and landed on my butt, my right hand landing with my palm down. My left wrist bent down, and the back of my hand hit the ground hard. I felt something snap in my left arm. I looked at my arm; from my wrist to my elbow was shaped like the letter S. I screamed, cradling my broken arm, and ran to the house, yelling for Mom.

Hearing me screaming and crying, Mom and Bob, our next-door neighbor, came running. He was a policeman. I was crying, looking at my misshapen arm.

Mom looked at it and said, "Maybe it's just dislocated."

Bob looked at Mom and replied, "No, Eve, it's broken."

Since Dad was at work, Bob took us to the hospital. On the way, Mom asked me if I could move my thumb. When I tried, a bone came sticking out of my arm. I was scared and crying. Mom put her arm around me, comforting me, and saying that everything would be okay; the doctors would be able to fix it.

At the hospital, I had x-rays taken. My arm was broken in three places. I needed surgery. While I was in the operating room, I looked over at the x-rays. This was the first time I saw that I had bones just like the skeleton in school. I remember thinking, *Yuck. I look like that inside?* Then I was put to sleep.

When I woke up, I was in a plaster cast from my fingertips to my armpit. Bob had left the hospital to go to work. Mom had called Dad while I was in surgery. When I woke up, he was there. I remembered that it was his birthday.

I said, "Happy birthday, Daddy."

He said, "Thank you," with a concerned look on his face. He knew the insurance wouldn't cover all the hospital bill. Some birthday present I gave him.

The good part of having a broken arm was that in school, all the tests I needed to take were written in true-and-false questions, since I was left-handed.

Every two weeks, I got out of school for the day, needing to go to the doctor to have my arm checked to see how it was healing. Dad took me for all my checkups. Afterwards, we'd go to the restaurant where my uncle worked to have lunch. I really enjoyed the attention I was getting. A couple of months later, my arm was fine.

One day, while playing in the field, I found a five-dollar bill. Wow; I was rich. I showed Hank the money and told him we were going to the drugstore, my treat. I loved my little brother, and I wanted to share my good fortune with him. The drugstore had a soda fountain bar, where they served food, sodas, and ice cream specialties.

Hank and I sat at the soda fountain. I told him to order anything he wanted. We both had hot dogs, French fries, and sodas. Then we each had an ice cream sundae with chocolate ice cream and marshmallow topping. Boy, were we full.

I wanted to buy Mom and Dad something with the money I had left. I bought Mom a nail brush and Dad a ten-cent cigar (there wasn't a law at the time prohibiting kids from buying tobacco products).

When we got home, I was so excited to give Mom and Dad the gifts. I gave Mom the nail brush, and she was really happy. She thanked me, and I was filled with pride. I gave Dad his cigar. He lit it up, took a couple of puffs, and put it out.

I asked, "Don't you like it?" not being able to hide my disappointment.

Dad answered, "Oh no, honey; it's just so special and good, I want to save it for later."

I believed him and felt better. Years later, I realized Dad didn't want to hurt my feelings. It must have tasted like an old burnt rug. Hank and I had told Mom and Dad that I found the money in the field, but we never told them how much I had found.

That winter, I wore a snowsuit that made me look like a boy.

I also wore a hat that I tucked my hair up inside. Carrying a snow shovel, I would walk to a different street, where I wasn't known. I would go door to door, asking if they wanted their sidewalks and driveways shoveled. I charged fifty cents for the sidewalk and a dollar for the driveway. I am sure they thought I was a boy, which was what I wanted. I knew that I wouldn't get work, being a girl. I made two or three dollars that day.

I missed having a girlfriend to play with. Sara was four years older, and she had different interests than me. Alone, I would play with my doll, sewing and making clothes for her, having a tea party, and pretending others were there, with just my doll and me. None of the girls from my school lived close by.

Mom and Dad had instilled a strong work ethic in us. We all had chores after school and on Saturday. Mom always said, "Get your work done first, then you can go out and play." We didn't get an allowance; as a family, all of us shared the work as we grew up. We all learned how to do the dishes, clean the house, and cook. The laundry and ironing were different than today. There were no permanent-press clothes. After washing and drying the clothes, they needed to be starched and dried again. Then sprinkled with water, rolled up, and let set for a day. Then the clothes were ironed. My brothers learned all the same chores as us girls did. In fact, my brother John became a chef in his adult life.

One Sunday when I was around eleven years old, Dad was very angry after coming home from church. The minister had addressed the congregation about getting a new pipe organ for the church; the church had an organ, but he said that the choir director felt it was inadequate. He said the church needed a pipe organ, and it cost three hundred thousand dollars. That was a tremendous amount of money, then.

The choir director told the minister if the church didn't get the pipe organ, he would leave. The minister didn't want to lose the choir director. The church would set up a special fund for the pipe organ. All of the congregation needed to contribute to the fund so that the choir director would stay. This was so against what Dad believed in, he never attended church again.

In 1955, Mom gave birth to a baby girl, Shelly. I had another sister; I was eleven years older than her.

Around twelve years old, I started to have different interests. I wanted the boys to like me as a girl, not as one of the guys. Their interest in girls was changing as well. They'd ask me how to get a girl they liked to be interested in them. I was always thought of as "good ol' Ellie, our buddy and pal."

I was going through an awkward stage. Mom was teaching us ballroom dancing at the time (she was a dancer when she was younger). John and I would go down to the rec room and practice all the different dances. We both loved it. I must say we were pretty good, doing the foxtrot, waltz, tango, cha-cha, and rock and roll. I liked being a girl.

Going into seventh grade, I was insecure and shy. At the same time, I was excited to be going to high school, which was seventh through twelfth grade.

Two girls in one of my classes came up to me, telling me that I needed to act more like a young lady. They said I needed to fix my hair and curl it. I wore it straight and tucked behind my ears. They also suggested I wear lipstick. I was deeply hurt but took their advice because I wanted to be liked and fit in. I paid more attention to how I dressed, fixing my hair and wearing makeup for the first time.

I was also told that if I wanted the boys to like me, I needed to let them win and think they were smarter and stronger than me.

All the girls had classes in sewing, cooking, and home economics, learning proper posture and sitting like a lady. There were no sports for girls to participate in. Of course, I also had classes in English, math, science, and history. We were educated in becoming housewives. Most of us would be married in a few years after graduation, we were told.

Acceptable occupations for women at the time were teachers,

librarians, nurses, and secretaries. If a woman went on to college, she was likely going to find a husband.

I was in the church choir from seventh grade to my senior year in high school. I loved singing in the choir. I also joined the youth group at church. Our youth group went to New York City to study different religions. New York City is a melting pot of religions from all over the world: different beliefs, different Gods, different ways humans came to be. I was so confused. None of this made any sense to me; it was frustrating. By the time I was around sixteen years old, I started to question whether God existed. I enjoyed history and science in school.

Santa Claus, the Easter Bunny, and the Tooth Fairy were all mythical beings, and I began to put God in that same category: mythical.

I could not see, touch, or feel Him, and I thought back to prayers when I had asked Him to help me. After all, the Bible said, "Ask and you shall receive." I didn't remember any prayer being fulfilled or answered.

I didn't tell my family or friends that I didn't believe in God anymore. I was afraid I would be rejected as a terrible person. I still sang in the choir. My friends at church and in school all believed in God. Of course, I was living a lie.

When I was fifteen, I got my first job at a local hospital. I was a tray girl, delivering the meals to the patients. Afterward, I would work in the kitchen, cleaning up.

I caught the bus after school to go to work. Our uniforms were blue and white pinstripes with a white collar, short sleeves, and white cuffs.

The hospital was different than today. This was 1959. There was a medical ward, a surgical ward, and maternity ward. The wards were large rooms with up to thirty-six beds in them. There were very few semiprivate rooms. Most of the private rooms were on one floor.

The hospital was remodeled several times over the years, while

I was there. By 1963, wards were gone, replaced by semiprivate and private rooms.

The kitchen was five-star, as far as I was concerned, so different from the hospital food today. There were chefs who prepared the main menus. Another chef prepared all the pastries, breads, and desserts, and there was a salad kitchen and a dietitian kitchen. Everything was made from scratch. The food was delicious.

Food trays were pleasing to the eye; trays had linen placemats, linen napkins, real silverware, glasses, dishes, coffee pots, and salt and pepper shakers. Everything was placed on the dishes and the tray with great care to look appetizing. There were college and high school students working in the kitchen. I really enjoyed working at the hospital.

After I graduated from high school, I stopped going to church, even though I was still a member. When someone who went to the church turned eighteen, they automatically became a member.

When I was in school, I loved science and history. I studied evolution, archeology (the study of ancient artifacts), anthropology, behavioral science, and paleontology (the study of ancient bones). I learned the history of early hominins, Neanderthals, and modern humans.

I read about different ancient civilizations: the Indus civilization in today's Pakistan, the Mesopotamian civilization, situated between the Tigris and Euphrates rivers, and the ancient Egyptian civilization; Chinese, Greek, and Roman civilizations also interested me.

I studied evolution and learned about animals that evolved from ancient predecessors. For example, the saber-tooth tiger died out, with the tiger of today evolving from him. Every ancient animal died off, with the animal of today evolving from them.

Why, then, were there still apes when we were supposed to have evolved from them? It didn't make any sense to me. I didn't believe it. The only animal still alive on earth with humans didn't follow evolution. Now, science has proven that we didn't evolve from apes; apes are a distant cousin. There is still no answer how humans evolved.

Science and history made more sense to me than the Bible.

Chapter 3
First Near-Death Experience

I left the hospital in 1963 and got a job at a discount store chain, with stores throughout the United States. I started out in the receiving room, ticketing merchandise, and worked my way up to cashier and customer service.

When I started working at the store, my boss was my future husband, although I didn't know it yet. In 1965, he asked me out on a date. We had a whirlwind romance and were married before the end of the year.

Pete didn't go to church, so I had a good excuse not to go myself. I never told him I didn't believe in God anymore.

Our marriage was rocky from the very start. I always allowed Pete to have it his way. I believed the husband was the head of the household. I needed to be the perfect wife.

We had been married about ten months when I said, "I love you," to him. I told him I loved him before this, but this time he said, "Don't tell me that. People don't know what the word means." I was deeply hurt. I was never able to tell my husband how I felt about him.

We bought our home in 1966. It was a lovely house with two bedrooms, a bath, a living room, and a nice rec room in the basement. French doors in the kitchen opened to a screened-in porch.

The neighbor next door was a retired professor. He had lots of books on ancient history such as the cave paintings in France, the

Stone Age, humans being nomadic and roaming from place to place before becoming settlers. I borrowed these books and read them. I also got a magazine on history delivered each month, and I read that from cover to cover.

Pete and I would go to museums while on vacation, learning about local history as well as global history.

After we were married about three and a half years, Pete said he didn't know if he wanted to be married anymore. This was the second time we separated. The first time was when we'd been married about two years. He was gone for about two months, the first time.

When he moved out this time, I was very scared; I felt lonely and empty. Weeks went by, and I didn't hear anything from Pete.

Sara was married. John had moved out on his own. Hank was in college in another city. Shelly was about fourteen. Mom was working full time. My family was busy with their own lives.

I was the first in my family to face a divorce. Marriage in my family was "til death do we part." I was scared and ashamed to talk to them.

I was working as an assistant pharmacist at a drugstore downtown; I took the bus to work.

At work, I would push my feelings of fear down inside. I pretended everything was fine and concentrated on doing my job.

I had gotten to know the neighbors across the street, Kurt and Hazel. They were around the age of my mom and dad. I could talk to them about what I was going through.

Like my dad, Kurt fought in World War II. Kurt had been shot in the head and still suffered with terrible pain from his wound. He received pain medication from the veteran's hospital.

About a month after John left, Kurt and Hazel invited me over for dinner. While we ate, I started to cry as I told them what happened and how scared and confused I was. Would I still be married or on my own? I loved John and didn't want a divorce. I hadn't slept for days, constantly worrying, crying, having a difficult time, shutting off my thoughts. I was an emotional wreck.

Kurt and Hazel were very concerned. All the emotions I had stuffed down for weeks, while working, came pouring out. Kurt left the room while Hazel held me in her arms, allowing me to cry.

Kurt came back in the room a few minutes later. He came up to me and gave me a hug. He had a tissue in his hand; opening it up, there were six pills inside. He explained they were a sedative and pain medication he got for his head injury. He said, "Take one about half an hour before going to bed. It'll help you get to sleep." He had given me enough for six days. I stayed a little while longer and then went home.

I got ready for bed. It was only 8:30, so I watched TV for a while. John and I seldom drank alcohol, only when we went out to dinner. We kept a bottle in the house in case we had company over. I remembered there was a bottle in the cabinet and made myself a drink of whiskey and Coke. I took a pill.

A half-hour went by. I was still wide awake. I thought to myself, *These pills don't seem as strong as Kurt said they were.* I made myself another drink and took another pill. I was still crying. I was afraid the pain would never stop. I took another pill and had another drink. By midnight, I had taken all six pills, along with six or seven drinks.

I don't remember going to bed. Somehow, I did get there.

Around 1:30 a.m., I was still asleep. I felt I was being lifted up, out of my body. I heard a fluttering sound. I heard music, so beautiful. I don't have the words to describe it. I was filled with peace and felt wonderful. I knew I was dying. I didn't see anything. I remember thinking, *I don't want to die. I have so many things I want to do and see. I am too young* (I was only twenty-five years old).

Somehow, I came to and sat up in bed. I was ice-cold to the touch. My skin sunk in on my arms when I touched them. I was terrified. I knew I had almost died. I was completely sober. Being so afraid, I stayed awake the rest of the night, afraid I might not come to the next time. When I look back now, I realized I had a strong will to live.

This was a lesson for me. Mixing alcohol and medication together could be deadly. There were no classes in school on drugs and alcohol, as there are today.

Although I was an assistant pharmacist, I still lacked the knowledge of mixing drugs and alcohol together. I'd get the prescription, type the label with the instructions on it, get the medication and bring it to the pharmacist. He would count out the medication and put it in the bottle and stick on the label. If there were any precautions or warnings added to the bottle, the pharmacist put them on. They were little stickers put on the bottle. I didn't pay attention once I typed the label.

Pete came home after being away almost three months.

After being home a few months, he decided he wanted to open his own business, a pet shop. He said I would manage it, while he kept his job.

He picked a pet shop because of my love for animals. I had pets my whole life: tropical fish, dogs, and rabbits. Of course, I gave in and said nothing.

I had to learn a lot: marketing, merchandising, inventory, ordering, and advertising. I learned a lot from Pete. I also realized that I needed to learn about the care, environment, gestation, and diseases of all of the animals and birds I sold.

After being open for about a year, I decided to add saltwater fish and studied marine biology. After three months, I had an aquarium with saltwater fish. The customers were amazed at the beautiful patterns and brilliant colors of the fish, compared to freshwater tropical fish.

The shop had three hundred aquariums, with thirty tanks of marine fish. We were the first store in the city to have saltwater fish.

The zoo bought supplies and food from us for one or two animals a month.

Fred Smith was the zoo director at that time. He'd ask me to take care of an animal or bird for a period of time whenever the zoo was building a new exhibit.

I took care of a kinkajou (commonly called a honey bear). Their face looks like a little bear with large eyes, having a yellowish-brown fur. They have a body and hands like a monkey, with a long prehensile tail. They are found from Mexico to South America.

We had a toucan (the Fruit Loops bird), a fruit-eating bird of tropical Central America, with brilliant coloring. I named him Knock Knock. When he wanted attention, he would knock his bill against the bars of his cage. Knock Knock loved me to scratch his head. He would purr like a kitten and rode on my shoulder while I worked around the store. He loved grapes. When he went back to the zoo, he was put in the children's exhibit because I trained him to be tame. I loved that little guy.

Back in the sixties, veterinarians didn't specialize in the care of wildlife like today.

One day, I got a call from Russ, the supervisor for the care of animals at the zoo. There had been a thunderstorm, and a hollow tree was struck by lightning and knocked down. Some kids found a nest of four baby screech owls in the tree. They brought the babies to the zoo. Since the zoo didn't have the staff to care for the owls, he asked me if I would raise them for the zoo.

All zoos have problems with rodents, due to the amount of food in outdoor exhibits. The zoo would release the owls in the park to help with the problem once I raised them.

I immediately went to the library to learn about the care of owls.

I needed to simulate the food they would eat in the wild: mice. I mixed up ground beef, ground-up liver, raw eggs, eggshells, and hair. The eggshells were like the bones from the mice. I got the hair from the barber shop next door to the store. I boiled the eggshells for twenty minutes to kill any bacteria. I would roll this mixture up into a ball. The owls would swallow it whole. In the wild, owls eat mice, hair, bones, and all.

Fifteen to twenty minutes after eating, they would excrete and regurgitate a ball of hair and eggshell. The hair and eggshell help with the digestion of their food. Birds have a crop to help grind their food. Once the owls digested their food, they regurgitated the hair and bones.

I kept the baby owls in an aquarium, with wooden chips for bedding, a screen top, and a lamp to keep them warm. They needed to be fed every three to four hours. I took the owls with me to the store and home for six weeks.

The owls grew stronger every day; I would take them into the living room to exercise their muscles and strengthen their wings. Putting one owl at a time on a wooden dowel, I'd move the dowel up and down, so they would start flapping their wings and building their muscles. Later, I put branches in the room, and they would fly from branch to branch.

Since owls excrete shortly after eating, I would wait until they went before bringing them into the living room.

Later, for the owls to acclimate being out in the environment, I took branches out on the screened in porch and left the owls there for the day. Later, I left them in there, day and night. They built their flying capabilities and adjusted to changes in the environment.

Teaching them to hunt was a challenge. I put a wooden dowel in the bathroom for the owls to perch on. I put four mice in the bathtub, so they couldn't escape, and left the owls in the bathroom with the door closed all day. It didn't take long for the three oldest; their natural instinct took over. The youngest never killed a mouse, though. She would only eat a dead mouse given to her.

I named them in the order that they were hatched. The eggs were laid one day at a time, so each chick was one day older than its next sibling. The oldest three had imprinted on their parents and were more aggressive. Their names were Godzilla, Hercules, and Sweetie Pie. The fourth one was named Squeaker.

Godzilla and Hercules were aggressive from the time I got them. Sweetie Pie became aggressive as time went on. They were only a few days old when the tree came down. I believe Squeaker was hatched the day the kids found them. She never became aggressive. She imprinted on me. I didn't know what sex they were; male and female owls look the same.

I just thought Squeaker was a girl because she was so loving. She loved to sit on my shoulder and cuddle next to my neck. She would make this cute little noise. I would pet her, and she'd fall asleep on my shoulder.

When they were about fourteen weeks old, I took them back to the zoo. The three oldest were released in the park. Squeaker went to the children's zoo because she was so tame. She wouldn't have survived in the park on her own.

I was working seven days a week. The store was open six days, closed Sunday. On Sunday, I would still go to the store. All of the fish, animals, and birds needed to be fed and their cages cleaned. The store was open from nine in the morning until nine at night. I had help working for me and would take off three nights a week. I would drive to the airport at eleven at night to pick up fish, birds, and animals; I'd take them back to the store and feed and water them.

Pete changed jobs and went to work for another company. Our marriage was falling apart.

In the summer of 1973, I told Pete that I wanted to close the pet shop. I was tired. I just wanted to work for someone else. It was one of the few times I had spoken up, saying what I wanted.

I was hoping by closing the store, I'd have more time to devote to our marriage and work out our problems. We had little time for each other. I was working eighty hours a week. We were becoming strangers.

In September, Pete said he wanted a divorce and moved out at the end of the month. I was working at the store when I was served the divorce papers. The store was closing, and I was selling the fish, animals, and birds. Later, I sold the equipment and inventory to other pet shops. The store was closed by the end of October.

I worked as a waitress at night, within walking distance from my home. I worked from 5 p.m. to 2 a.m.

I still loved Pete and wanted to save our marriage. Someone suggested I get counseling. They said a church would be able to help me. Because I was supporting myself and only had a small income, I could not afford a therapist on my own. I was still listed as a member of the church, even though I hadn't attended in over ten years. I called the minister, and he made arrangements for me to go to counseling. The cost was based on my income.

After seeing a therapist a few times, I was put in group therapy. The therapist asked each of us why we were there. When he came to me, I said, "I want to learn how to save my marriage."

His response was, "We are not here to help save a marriage; we are here to help people fix themselves."

I was angry. I still stayed, figuring there might be something I could learn that might save my marriage, anyway.

Pete and I were talking, so I was hopeful we would get back together.

In December, a week before the divorce was final, he asked me to attend his company's Christmas party. This would be our first date since separating. He divorced me on a Friday, and our first date was the next day, Saturday night.

We dated for about four and a half months. One night, I realized our marriage was over, and I needed to move on with my own life. That was the last night we were together.

Chapter 4
A Life of Change

I stayed in therapy, although I didn't take it seriously. After all, I only wanted to save my marriage. The marriage was over. I don't know why I stayed at the time.

There were eight to twelve in our group. People would share about a mistake they made, and I'd jump all over them. I was critical and judgmental. What they did was wrong, and I needed to let them know it.

After all, I was a good person, sweet and kind. Of course, that's how I saw myself. Having a low self-worth, I learned a long time ago not to let anyone know about my mistakes, weaknesses, faults, or defects. So I was critical of others' errors, since I couldn't accept my own.

A woman in our group was going through a divorce at the same time as me. Fergie was years older than me. She was angry, nervous, always shaking. She also wanted to save her marriage. We talked a lot and both had the same goal. Her husband was divorcing her as well.

In the spring of 1975, I noticed a big change in Fergie. Her divorce had been final for over a year. She was calm and tranquil. I wondered what had happened to help her change. She left the group shortly after that. I gave up on therapy and left shortly after she did.

I met a nice guy named Dan. He was tall and ruggedly handsome. I really liked him. After we'd been dating for over a month, we made

27

plans to go on a picnic. The day before our date, Dan called to tell me his former girlfriend came to see him. They were going to see if they could rebuild their relationship. He apologized and said he still had feelings for her.

I was deeply hurt. I thought to myself, *What is wrong with me?* I looked back at how many times I'd been rejected by men. My boyfriend in high school, a boyfriend after school, my first husband, and now Dan.

I decided to take a look at myself. I remember the first time I took responsibility for being wrong. I was sitting in my rec room alone and spoke aloud, admitting what I'd done. I had a sharp pain in my head and saw a blue light. I'd woken a part of myself for the first time. I felt so relieved.

The first time I talked about my hatred, I was afraid to talk to another person, in person. I called Fergie on the phone. If she told me I was wrong and terrible, I was going to hang up the phone.

I told her what I'd done. I don't remember what I said. I was scared and crying.

I said, "Please don't tell me I'm bad."

Fergie answered, "I admire your honesty."

From that time on, I started to change, with the help of Fergie. I now understood a lot of what I had heard in therapy.

I still hadn't told her I didn't believe in God. In 1982, I did.

In January 1976, I was hired by a food manufacturing corporation as a sales rep. I called on supermarkets, grocery stores, and distribution centers. The position required a person with a college degree in business management and marketing. I only had a high school degree, but I had owned and operated my own business for over five years. When I got this job, I felt so proud of myself.

Part of therapy was understanding my emotions and paying attention to what I was feeling. Emotions are neither good or bad. Staying in touch with my feelings and trusting them took awhile.

As time went on, I grew mentally and emotionally. I learned

to trust my emotions. I had them for a reason. Because I was more understanding of my own emotions, I was sensitive to and understood other people's feelings. I developed a sensitivity, even with my surroundings.

Chapter 5
Evil Experience Past Homestead

In the late 1970s, I needed a dress altered. I found an ad for a seamstress and called to make an appointment to bring the dress to her at her house. She lived on Knapp, way out past the East Beltline.

It was a Saturday morning at the end of March. The sky was gray with drizzling rain, and it was chilly.

Driving east on Knapp, I came to the corner of Knapp and the East Beltline. I noticed a little church on the corner to my left. It looked like a church that was built in the 1800s. There was a historical sign in front. I thought to myself, *I want to stop on my way back to learn the history of that little church.* But I never did.

Crossing the East Beltline, still on Knapp, the road changed to gravel and dirt. I drove down a hill. A while later, I could see a bridge up ahead. The bridge, with guardrails, went over a swamp. To the left, past the bridge, was an old homestead. A stone fireplace and chimney were still partially standing. A path was overgrown where wagons had gone up to the house and past to where the barn probably stood.

As I drove over the bridge, I felt something evil surround me. I was terrified. I could feel hate, anger, fear, and pain all around me, and I could hardly breathe. I drove faster. As I passed the property line of the old farm, I felt the evil stop, as if it could not pass the property line. I was scared and confused.

After I dropped off my dress to the seamstress, I drove the long way home. I was afraid to go past that place again.

When I went to pick up my dress a week later, I once again drove the long way to her house and back to mine, in order to avoid the old homestead.

I had a lot going on at the time. I had been promoted to area accounts manager, calling on major accounts and having a lot more responsibility.

My sister Shelly was getting married at the time. Helping her with her wedding and my new responsibilities at work, I forgot about the experience with the old farm.

A couple of months later, Mom called, wanting to go to yard sales. I said yes. Mom and Dad had built a home on the river. They sold the house I had grown up in since I was eight years old. She picked me up about 8:30 in the morning.

I enjoyed being with Mom. I was close to her, even when I was young. No matter what I was going through, Mom was always there.

It was a beautiful sunny day. Mom had the newspaper with the yard sales she wanted to go to marked. We'd already gone to several sales. I wasn't paying particular attention to where we were going. I was reading the ads and discussing what each yard sale had listed for sale.

She had passed the East Beltline. We were on Knapp Street. When I looked up, I noticed we were almost to the bridge that went over the swamp, and the old farm was up ahead on the left.

When we went over the bridge, I felt surrounded by evil, hate, anger, fear, and pain once again. I froze. I looked at Mom and said, "Something terrible and evil is here; can you feel it?"

Mom looked at me with concern and said, "No, honey; Ellen, you're as white as a ghost."

I was trembling. I was so scared. I said, "Please drive fast past this place."

Just like before, as we passed the property line, what I felt stopped, as if it wouldn't go any farther.

I begged her not to go past that place again on the way home. We drove to the town where Mom was born and grew up. We visited her girlfriends she had grown up with, and we had lunch with them.

Then she drove back to my place, taking a different route. I kissed Mom and told her I loved her as she dropped me off.

Being busy with work, I forgot about the old farm. That summer, I often went to see Mom and Dad. I'd go swimming in the river. We ate outside at the picnic table. Sometimes, I would go fishing. It was peaceful there, and I could rest after a busy week with work.

Summer passed into fall. With the seasons change, I was busy with work, thinking up new merchandising ideas and setting up displays for Thanksgiving and then Christmas. I had sales presentations and promotions. I worked long hours right up until Christmas.

Christmas was a big get-together with the family at Mom and Dad's house. The family had really grown. Sara had five children. Hank was married with two children. Shelly was pregnant with her first child. John and I were still single. We had a full house.

Mom made Christmas special, with lots of food and presents. The kids were excited with each package they opened. I enjoyed Christmas, being with my family, not for the real meaning of Christmas.

In February of the next year, I was reading the Sunday newspaper. I always read the ads for the week on grocery stores and supermarkets. I enjoyed having a cup of coffee and reading the paper.

With Martin Luther King Jr.'s birthday celebrated, there was a section of black history stories. Being interested in history, I read them.

One Sunday, there was a section on the history of Michigan and the Underground Railroad. There were eight to ten stories altogether.

Many people do not realize that in the early to mid-1800s, Michigan was an important stop along the Underground Railroad. This system was designed to move escaped slaves north toward freedom; it was called a railroad because they used much of the terminology from the newly developing railway system. "Conductors" were the people who helped runaway slaves move along the railway. The safe houses, where slaves could rest, were called "stations," and the escaped slaves were referred to as "baggage." Northerners would hide runaway slaves in their homes or barns, until they were sure it was safe to move them to the next station.

This system was built upon secret codes from the Bible as well. For example, "the Promised Land" or "Canaan" referred to Canada, where slavery had been abolished. The "River Jordan" was really the Ohio River, which you needed to cross in order to reach the Promised Land. Because Michigan, one of the states that border Canada, was often the last stop along this escape route.

The Fugitive Slave Law was passed in 1850, allowing slave catchers to enter free states, hunt down runaway slaves, and return them to their plantations. The slave hunters were paid a handsome bounty for slaves, dead or alive. The bounty hunters were sometimes instructed to kill certain slaves who were troublemakers or repeated runaways. Their bodies would be brought back to the plantation and hung up for display by the slave quarters in order to terrify the rest of the slaves. This would happen to anyone who tried to run away. The dead slave was worth more as a deterrent.

One of the stories told of an incident that happened where eight escaped slaves, referred to as cargo, were delivered by wagon in the dark to the church on the corner of Knapp and the East Beltline. They were hidden at the church until they could be moved to the next station en route to Canada. Groups of slaves were put in wagons and moved in the night to a farm on Knapp, east of the East Beltline. The farm was owned by a Quaker. The slaves were hidden in a cellar under the barn.

Later that night, the farm was raided by slave catchers. The fugitive slaves were discovered in the cellar under the barn. The slave catchers took two of the male slaves and killed them. They took their bodies and put them on the back of horses. The rest of the slaves were shackled and put into wagons, and all were taken back south.

There was a hand-drawn map showing the church on the corner of Knapp and the East Beltline. I froze when I read the story and looked at the map.

The farm was in the location of the old farm with the stone fireplace and chimney still partially standing. I questioned what I was sensing that horrible situation that happened over one hundred twenty years ago when I went past the old farm. I will always remember how terrified I was going past that place. The route that the slaves took was the same route that I took. I wondered, was this the same farm? I will never know for sure.

Chapter 6
The Angel

I'd grown from the person I was when I was married, taking responsibility for my thoughts, actions, and decisions, my weaknesses and strengths. I was honest about my hate, anger, jealousy, and greed.

There were times I was overwhelmed and discouraged. This was one of those days, where I wanted to cry hysterically. While I was working, I would put my thoughts and feelings aside in order to do my job.

On that day, I was calling on supermarkets and grocery stores in another city. Grocery stores are independently owned, small chains, or just one store. They had carry-out service. A bagger or stock boy would bag a customer's groceries and carry them out to their car. Most baggers wore a white apron.

I also called on a supermarket chain that didn't have carry-out service; they had drive-up service. The bagger would pack their groceries in a shopping cart, take them to a designated area, and the customer would drive up to the designated area. Then the bagger would load the groceries into their car for them. At this supermarket chain, all employees wore a white shirt and a dark gold vest. The meat department employees wore white coats.

I had just finished calling on one of their stores; this was my last call of the day. I was sitting in my car in their parking lot.

It was a beautiful sunny day. My windows were open. I had set my emotions aside all day. I finally broke down. I was crying uncontrollably and felt overwhelmed.

I heard a voice say, "Can I help?"

I looked to my side, and standing next to my car was a young man. He had a blue plaid shirt on with a white apron. His eyes were full of compassion and concern. There was an aura around him. I felt unworthy to be in his presence. I sensed that he wasn't from this earth.

I looked down and said, "No, thank you."

When I looked up, he was gone. In a blink of an eye, he was gone. I was stunned and confused. I jumped out of the car and looked everywhere. No one can move that fast. Was he an angel? I questioned what just happened.

I knew he wasn't from this store. All employees wore white shirts and dark gold vests. There was no carry-out service at this store, either.

I tried to come up with a logical and realistic answer but could not. I didn't want to believe what just happened. God and angels don't exist. *It's not real,* I told myself. I decided that I wouldn't think about it again. Years later, I knew he was an angel who came to help me at that time.

In 1982, Fergie asked me to go to church with her. I respected her for having her own beliefs, and out of my respect for her, I said I would go.

After going to church, we went back to her house; I told her that I accepted Jesus did live. He probably was just a nice man who cared about people. But I didn't believe that he was the Son of God.

"I don't believe in God," I told her.

She answered, "Now you will find the truth."

I didn't think much of her statement at that time.

Later that year, Fergie moved to the West Coast to live with her daughter.

Chapter 7
The Devil

My life went on as usual. In time, I lost touch with Fergie. Long-distance phone calls cost more than I could afford. Writing lacked the emotional response. Fergie, who was my sounding board, allowed me to admit when I was wrong and to come up with my own answers. I missed my friend, who was never judgmental.

In April 1983, my niece, Leah, came to visit and stay overnight. She was sixteen years old at the time. We had gone shopping and went out to lunch. We had a real good time. After going back to my house, I was reading history and Leah was listening to some religious records that she had brought with her.

After several hours of listening to religious music and sermons, I asked her to please play something else.

She asked, "Aunt Ellen, don't you like religious music?"

I said, "No, I don't believe in God or the devil. If the devil exists, he can have me. I believe in science and history." I changed the subject.

We had dinner, did the dishes, and watched a movie on television. We went to bed about eleven o'clock that night. Leah slept with me, since I only had one full-size bed. She had stayed overnight before and sometimes would hit me with her hand when she turned over in bed.

I was lying on my stomach and just starting to doze off. I felt a cold cloud starting at my feet and slowly moving up, engulfing my whole body. I felt something evil crawl into my ear. I heard the most diabolical laughter inside my head. Terrified, I screamed, jumped out of bed, and ran into the living room.

I was shouting, "Get out," and slapping the side of my head.

Leah came running into the room and turned a light on. She was crying and saying, "I'm sorry, Aunt Ellen. I didn't mean to hit you."

I said, "No, honey, you didn't hit me."

I explained what had happened. She was crying, so I asked, "Honey, why are you crying? You didn't do anything."

She answered, "Because there is blood running down your neck."

I put my hand to my neck, and there was blood. I went into the bathroom, got a washcloth, and washed the blood off. I thought maybe I had scratched myself when I was slapping the side of my head. There were no cuts or scratches. The blood was coming from my ear. I told Leah, maybe I slapped the side of my head too hard and caused it to bleed, but I knew I hadn't.

I tried to reassure her that it was just a dream, but deep down inside, I knew it wasn't.

I blocked the experience out of my mind and said, "Let's just go back to bed; I am fine."

We got up the next morning as if nothing had happened. We made breakfast and ate, all the while laughing and giggling. She was talking about school and boys. I could relate to when I was in school. The conversation was light and fun. Later, I took Leah home.

When I got back home, I did some house cleaning. When I was through, I got a magazine and went out on the porch. I was so relaxed. I sat and read, enjoying the beautiful sunny day on my porch.

Later, after dinner, I got ready for bed. I watched television in my nightgown, and around ten o'clock, I went to bed.

I was laying on my back with my hands up under my head, thinking about the proposal I would be presenting the next day at work.

Something caught my eye. I looked over at the door, and standing in the doorway was the most beautiful man I had ever seen. He had dark curly hair with the most captivating, beautiful smile. He was dressed in a white suit, black shirt, and white tie.

I was attracted and drawn to him. I wanted to go with him. Oh, how I wanted to go with him. In the pit of my stomach, I felt a small fear, saying, "Don't go, don't go." I knew who he was, yet I still wanted to go. He was so intriguing.

He came closer and sat down next to me on the bed. When I looked into his eyes, I saw emptiness. There were no emotions, just blackness. I quickly closed my eyes, as I was scared. I screamed, "Go away, I hate you." I heard a blood-curdling laugh.

When I opened my eyes, he was gone. I felt so relieved, and I fell asleep.

Chapter 8
Being Saved

The next day, I felt fine. I was sure he was gone after I told him to go away. Which he did, I thought.

Being Monday, I was busy with work all day. After work, I went out to dinner. I seldom cooked, only when I had company. I had cooked for years almost every day. I enjoyed the freedom of cooking only if I wanted to, which was seldom.

After dinner, I drove home and went into my office. I worked on reports for about an hour and then watched TV for a while. I went to bed around ten o'clock. Being a weeknight, I would have to get up early for work the next day.

As I lay there, I was scared. I was being tormented. I saw the faces of humans in agony, bloodied faces with blackened-out eyes. I heard hysterical screaming, crying, and weeping. There was a sound of chains rattling, the cracking of a whip, and the roar of a beast gnashing his teeth. The sounds were deafening. I saw faces of evil demons; it didn't matter if my eyes were open or closed.

I was terrified and angry at the same time. I screamed, "Go away. I hate you, and I don't want you in my life." Then I would hear a defiant, horrifying laughter. The visions and sounds went on and on, all night.

This torment went on for seven or eight nights. I was exhausted and short-tempered. I was getting little sleep and struggled doing my job. I wanted this nightmare to end.

I had gotten to know Fred, an employee at a supermarket a few blocks from my home. I'd shopped at this market for years, and they were also a client for my job.

Fred worked at this store. He was a neighbor and an ordained minister. Out of desperation, I stopped at the store on my way home. I asked Fred to please come over after work.

When Fred arrived, I shared everything, from the statement I had made about not believing in God and the devil and that I had said that if the devil exists, he could have me. That very night, something evil crawled into my ear. The next night, Satan appeared before me in his beauty. I shared about the nights of torture I had been experiencing and how I hated Satan and his evil buddies. I told him how I yelled and screamed that I hated him and that he should go away. But they didn't leave, and I couldn't make the torment stop.

Fred said, "Ellen, you are not strong enough to get rid of him. There is only one who has the power, and that is Christ. You need to pray and ask him to get rid of him."

I thought to myself, *This is stupid. I can get rid of him. I am in charge.*

Fred asked me to get down on my knees and pray with him. He said, "Ask Christ to get rid of him, Ellen."

I got down on my knees, but I was angry and defiant. I said, "God, get rid of Satan," and then looked at Fred and said, "See, nothing happened."

Fred shook his head in disappointment, and he left.

Later that night, when I went to bed, I experienced the same tormenting. As I lay there, for the first time, I realized if Satan exists, then so must Christ.

I prayed with reverence, "Dear Lord, now I understand that I need your help. Would you, please, get rid of Satan?"

I felt all my anger and fear leave. I felt his presence. I was filled with peace and love. I felt him protecting me and said, "Thank you, Lord."

I saw a cloud of red smoke, and then it disappeared. I was at peace, and finally, I fell asleep.

The next day, I thought about the cloud of red smoke. I was a little troubled. Maybe the red smoke meant that Satan might still come back.

On my way home from work the next day, I stopped at the supermarket and asked Fred if he would come over after work again.

When Fred came, I told him how wrong I had been. I'd prayed for help, and Christ came to protect me. I told him about the red smoke and how it disappeared. I was scared that Satan might come back. I thought of the red cloud of smoke and associated it with him.

Fred said, "Maybe, I don't know. Maybe the cloud of red smoke stood for the blood that Christ shed for you."

I realized Fred was right. I thanked him, and he left. Alone, I cried and understood how wrong I had been for many years.

I recalled Fergie's statement: "Now you'll discover the truth." She was right; I found out the most terrible way possible.

Chapter 9
Miracle by Two Men

The very next Sunday, I went to church. I'd never been to this kind of church before. When I walked in, Reverend Don and his wife, Sharon, greeted me. I was amazed at how friendly they both were. After the service, Reverend Don asked me for my phone number. I was surprised he called that very afternoon and came over. He invited me to come to church next Sunday to meet the other members.

As it turned out, two members of the church had gone to high school with me. After going for a few weeks, I joined the choir. I enjoyed going to this church. We were like a family, caring for each other. If a member was in need, we were there to help. All members helped take care of the church and the grounds. If painting needed to be done, the church supplied the paint, and the members supplied the labor.

Reverend Don never talked about money matters in the service. Service was for the worship of God; it was so different from the church I grew up with.

After months attending church and getting to know Reverend Don, I asked him to come to my home after service. I needed to share how I became a believer again.

I told him about the cold cloud starting at my feet and engulfing my body; something evil crawled in my ear.

He asked, "Why not your mouth, your nose?"

I was startled and changed the subject.

After he left, I put myself in his shoes. I would have reacted in the same way in the past. Not having experienced what the other person had, I'd have been afraid of the unknown. I would have been defensive and sarcastic. I understood he was only scared. Since then, I've been very selective who I share my spiritual experiences with.

Jack and I dated for a few years, off and on, four or five times per year.

In August 1983, we went camping in Canada for the car endurance races. We camped next to the racetrack with Dick and Jan, friends of Jack. I had a wonderful time and gained two new friends.

Jack and I weren't meant for each other. We parted as friends.

Dick, Jan, and I stayed in touch. In November, Dick and Jan came to my home for a visit. They lived in Harper Woods, a suburb of Detroit.

As the months went by, I became bored with my job. I needed something new. I wanted to sell something more challenging.

After looking for months, I found a position in Detroit. This was a consulting firm specializing in training in international quality standards. I accepted the position.

I would be responsible for calling on the US government and Fortune 500 manufacturing companies to integrate training programs.

I sold the house where I'd lived in for seventeen years. I was excited about the new position as a sales executive. At the same time, I grieved leaving my home.

While I was busy packing, I was listening to the local news station. There was a report about a couple in the Detroit area getting people to stop on the expressway, beating them up, and robbing them. I was only half-listening at the time.

I found an apartment in Grosse Pointe Park. It was a brick house built in the twenties or thirties. It had two apartments; mine was upstairs. The craftsmanship was exquisite. The living room had a marble fireplace. Above the fireplace was a beautiful hand-carved ship from the seventeenth century. I love nautical themes. My coffee table is a ship's wheel with a glass top. The rug under the table is a compass rose. I had an aquarium (and still do).

In June of 1984, I said goodbye to my family and friends. Some of my friends from church helped me pack the truck. Don from church volunteered to drive the rental truck to my apartment and back, to save me the extra cost of leaving the truck in Detroit.

Don, Dick, and Jan helped me move in. We all went out for a late lunch, my treat.

I hugged Don, thanked him, and said, "Tell everyone I'll see them when I come home for a visit."

The next two weeks, I was busy learning technical consulting, training, and materials the company offered to industrial accounts, taking classes in international quality standards (commonly called ISO-9000), statistical process control, quick tooling change, synchronous manufacturing, and quality function deployment.

After three weeks, I began working on accounts.

One day, I had a client come to the office. I then took him out to dinner, getting to know him and what his company needed. About ten at night, I drove him back to his hotel.

I drove back to the expressway, the on-ramp was closed; they were doing repairs. I followed the detour signs until there were no more signs. I was lost.

I ended up in an area that no person should be in during the day, let alone after dark. This was where drug deals and prostitution took place.

I drove around for hours. I was scared and trembling. I stopped at a red light. I was crying. I prayed, "Dear Lord, I am lost and scared. I need your help. Please help me find my way home."

A few seconds later, I heard a car pull up next to me.

My window was open. (I was still naive about having my window open while driving around in Detroit.) I heard a man's voice say, "Ma'am?"

I looked over. Two African American men were in the other car. I immediately went to roll the window up. I was so scared.

One of the men said, "Ma'am, we just want to help you. You're lost."

I was stunned. How did they know? They weren't there when I was praying. They drove up next to me afterwards.

The same man said, "If you'll tell us where you need to go, we will get you there."

I was still scared. Both had kind and concerned expressions. I told them where I lived. He said, "Follow us; we know the way."

I was hopeful and apprehensive at the same time. After what seemed like forever, I finally recognized some streets. They pulled up in front of my house. I parked my car, got out, and went over to their car to thank them.

One said, "We'll wait until you are safe to the door."

When I got to the front door, I turned and waved. They drove away. I never saw them again.

I thanked God that night for the help he sent me. I know they weren't there when I prayed, asking for help. How did they know I was lost? I believe God sent them.

Chapter 10
Couple Trying to Stop Me on the Highway

It took some time getting to know the city and become familiar with the area,. Even grocery shopping was different. Where I lived, there were no supermarkets. There was a farmer's market, a butcher shop, and Italian and Greek stores. There were bakeries of different countries. It was a regular smorgasbord of stores from all nations.

Saturday, I would grocery shop for a couple of hours, going from store to store and trying new foods. I loved it. All of these stores were just a block or two from my apartment.

Dick, Jan, and I would go to Greek-Town for the wonderful Greek restaurants. The food was fabulous. I was meeting new people in the neighborhood and making new friends. Jim, a doctor, specialized in cancer. Carol was a nurse. Both became good friends.

I decided to get some fish for my aquarium. One day, I asked the couple next door, George and Ida, where there was a pet shop. I drove down the street they said it was on but couldn't find it. I must have driven two miles; I noticed the area was getting run down, so I decided to turn around and go back. When I made a left turn into an out-of-business gas station, five or six guys encircled my car. They were holding up little plastic bags of drugs, trying to sell them to me. I was glad I had my windows up. I immediately got out of there. Oh, the lessons I would learn while living in the Detroit area.

The first of August, Dick, Jan, and I went to Canada for the car endurance races. The racetrack was about eight hours from Detroit. Dick and Jan left Friday morning to get our campsite next to the racetrack.

I needed to work that day, but my boss let me leave early. I had packed my car the night before with my camping gear. Leaving from work, I headed for the Windsor Tunnel and took the 401 expressway in Canada. I was heading east and had a long way to go.

I got to the campsite at eleven thirty that night. Dick and Jan were waiting up for me. They helped me unpack and set up my tent. Then we all went to bed.

We got up at six the next morning. Cars were already warming up on the racetrack. The cars with turbo engines were loud. The roar of the engines and the speed of the cars was exciting.

The weekend went by fast. Dick and Jan were staying until Monday morning, having Monday off. I needed to leave Sunday to be back at work on Monday.

I left around four in the afternoon, getting to the Windsor Tunnel around midnight. I got on the expressway heading west.

A while later, a car pulled up next to me on my left. They were honking their horn, trying to get my attention. I hesitated at first to look over at them. Then I thought, *I'm okay*.

I rolled down the window and looked over. There was a man and a woman in the car. They yelled, "You have a flat tire. Follow us, and we'll help you change it."

I said, "Okay, thank you."

They pulled in front of me and went some distance. They put their turn signal on to pull off to the side of the expressway, under the viaduct.

I was getting ready to pull off to the side as well when I heard a loud male voice shout, "Don't stop."

I was startled but I kept driving. I looked over at the passenger seat. It sounded like he was sitting right next to me, but no one was there.

Then I thought my tire must be getting low on air, because I couldn't feel a flat. My exit came up. I was tired and I thought, *I think I can make it home. I'll change it in the morning.* I took my exit instead of stopping.

I got up early and got dressed to go out to change the tire and unpack the car. I walked around the car twice, looking at the tires. There was no flat; none of the tires were low on air. I froze with fear. This couple had been up to something bad. I could have been robbed, beaten, or something even worse.

I would have stopped too, if it wasn't for the voice shouting, "Don't stop."

Was God protecting me? I believe he was. I thanked him for watching over me.

Once in a while, after work, I would buy the newspaper on my way home. When I got home, I liked to have a cup of coffee and read the news. The first thing I would do when I got home was kick off my shoes, get out of my business clothes, and put on something comfortable. I would sit with my coffee, relax, and read the paper.

A month or so after the incident with the couple trying to get me to stop on the expressway, I sat down to relax. I unfolded the newspaper and looked at the front page. There were pictures of a man and a woman. My stomach knotted up. There was something familiar about them. Then I read the headline. It was "Expressway Couple Caught in Toledo, Ohio."

This couple had been operating in the Detroit area for months. I had heard about them when I was listening to the news while I was packing to move but had forgotten about it. They had robbed and beaten eight or nine people and killed an elderly couple. When it got too hot for them in Detroit, they went to Toledo and tried the same scam, getting people to stop on the expressway.

They had been caught. The police in several states had been looking for them. I thought about that couple who tried to get me to stop on the expressway. I only saw their faces for less than a minute, in the dark. I was scared when I looked at their pictures. I hadn't even read the headline yet.

Was this the same couple? I don't know. About a month had passed since the incident. I would have stopped if it wasn't for the loud voice shouting, "Don't stop."

Chapter 11
Cancer; God Saved My Life Two Times

In October, my friends and I planned a Halloween party. Everyone wore costumes. Friends invited other friends. We rented a banquet room. There were around a hundred of us. There was lots of food, with everyone bringing a dish to pass.

We all danced the night away. I was a flapper from the Roaring Twenties. Dr. Jim dressed as a vampire. I had a wonderful time.

Christmastime came, and I went home to be with my family. I arrived several days before Christmas, helping Mom with the baking and cooking. Mom, Dad, and I spent some time together before the whole family came.

During the winter, Dr. Jim and I would go ice skating with other friends. Jim and I were just friends, no romantic involvement. We would go out to dinner and shows, and meet for coffee sometimes; we each paid our own way.

In May of 1985, Jim and I had plans to go out to dinner. I called him earlier that day to cancel our date, telling him about the stomach cramps and heavy flow I was having with my period.

He was concerned and came over later that afternoon. He asked when was the last time I had been to a doctor and had a pap smear test. I told him that it had been over six years. My old doctor had died, and I never got a new doctor. He said I should see a doctor right away and have a pap test. Since he had been out of private practice for years, he wasn't able to recommend a doctor.

I found a doctor who was an OB/GYN, Dr. Jenn, and made an appointment for the first of June, a Friday. I went in and had a pap test.

Later Monday morning, I received a phone call at work from the doctor's office. The nurse said I needed to come in to see the doctor that afternoon. I told her that I couldn't leave work without knowing why. She said my pap test came back, and it was serious. I told my boss, and he immediately said I could leave.

Dr. Jenn told me my test showed signs of cancer. I needed to have a biopsy and a mammogram done.

I had called Jim earlier and told him that my pap test was serious. We met for coffee after I saw the doctor. Jim explained to me the pap test readings: 1 or 2 meant normal; 3 indicated an infection; 4 or above indicated signs of cancer; 5 meant cancer for sure.

My reading was a 4.3. Jim explained that the biopsy would assess the severity of the cancer. If cancer cells were just on the surface of the cervix, they would freeze them. The cells would die. If the cancer had grown into the muscle tissue, I'd have two options.

Option one: They would cut the cancerous tissue out and follow up with radiation. The consequence of the radiation was that it would harden the walls of the vagina, and I wouldn't be able to have an intimate relationship with a man. Option two was a hysterectomy.

Two weeks later, after the biopsy and mammogram, Dr. Jenn said that my mammogram was fine. The biopsy, however, showed that the cancer had spread into the muscle of the cervix.

Dr. Jenn presented the same two options that Jim had explained to me. I considered the consequences of the radiation. I still thought I might get married someday, so I decided on the hysterectomy.

I told her, "I don't want to hear that the cancer is back three to five years from now."

She agreed that it was the best option.

The surgery was set for July 5.

Mom and Shelly came on Sunday, July 4. I needed to be at the hospital later that afternoon for tests before the surgery the next day. Since the surgery was scheduled for eight o'clock in the morning, I would be staying overnight.

That morning, we went to Windsor, Canada, to see the city. They had never been there before. We went shopping and later went out to lunch.

All the while, Mom and Shelly kept the conversation light. They knew I was nervous. When they took me to the hospital later, we were all nervous. They both kissed me and reassured me that everything was going to be okay. They would be back the next morning; they were staying at my place overnight.

They arrived before I left for surgery. I had already received a sedative, and then I was taken into surgery.

The next thing I remember, I was in my hospital room. Mom and Shelly were there. I was feeling the effects of being sedated, coming to and falling back asleep.

Mom said that everything went fine. I would be in the hospital for seven days and go home on the eighth day. They would come and get me then. Both kissed me and left.

Every few hours, all through the night and the next day, I received a pain shot. By Tuesday night, I told the nurse that I didn't want any more pain shots. I was black and blue where I got the shots, and it hurt. Being drugged, I couldn't function and was so dizzy, I couldn't think straight. I was sick to my stomach from the shots.

Wednesday morning, I was able to think more clearly, being off the pain medication. I was sick to my stomach, nauseated, and weak, with chills all day.

That night, I couldn't sleep. I lay there, looking at the clock on the wall, opposite from my bed. It was eleven o'clock.

I was weak and felt as if I was going to throw up, but I couldn't. I felt my energy leaving me, my life fading. I tried to reach for the button to call the nurse but couldn't move. I tried to call out for help but wasn't able to. I was getting weaker and weaker, and I knew I was dying.

I prayed, "Dear Lord, it's okay if you want me to be with you. It's okay if you want me to live. I need your help."

I instantly felt His presence and the fulfillment of His caring and His loving touch. He cradled me in His arms. I was filled with peace and comfort. I felt my energy come back and fell asleep in His loving arms.

The next few days, I was weak and had chills. Dr. Jenn never came in to see me in the hospital after my surgery.

Sunday, another doctor came to remove the drainage tube from my stomach. I was in extreme pain when she pulled the tube out. I heard the nurse tell the doctor that I had a low-grade fever all this past week.

I still felt weak. Mom and Shelly were coming tomorrow to take me home first thing in the morning. I wanted to go home and be with Mom, who would take care of me. I didn't tell the nurse that I didn't feel well.

That night, as I lay in bed, I felt my life draining away again. I prayed for God to help me. He came to me as he did before, cradling me in his arms. I was filled with his love, just as before. I fell asleep in his arms.

Mom and Shelly came early the next morning. Dr. Jenn said I had a low-grade fever and that I needed to take an antibiotic. I was allowed to go home and would return to see the doctor in two weeks. Mom and Shelly had packed a suitcase for me before, so we could leave right from the hospital.

We had a long drive ahead of us; it was about four hours to Mom and Dad's home.

We stopped in Fowlerville around 11:30 for lunch. I wasn't very hungry but was relieved that we had stopped so I could rest. I could feel every bump on the expressway.

Just east of Ionia, I felt something wet on my stomach. I lifted up my dress, and liquid was leaking out of the hole where the drainage tube had been.

I said, "It's nothing, probably from bouncing around in the car."

We dropped Shelly off at her home, and Mom and I drove home. Dad was glad to see us. Later that afternoon, I lay down and fell asleep.

Mom woke me up. She had made a wonderful dinner of meatloaf, mashed potatoes, and fresh green beans. I ate very little, but everything tasted good. I slept in the living room. The sofa had a rollout bed. I still felt weak.

When I got up the next morning, I felt better. I got dressed. It was a beautiful sunny day. Later, I took a blanket and went outside. I lay down in the sun on a chaise longue and covered myself with the blanket. I felt a little chilled. I fell asleep and woke up late in the afternoon.

That night, we had dinner and watched TV. I was tired and fell asleep around nine o'clock.

The next morning, I had coffee with Mom and Dad, and we talked about the day. Dad mentioned that if I was up to it, we would go for a boat ride later in the afternoon. He went out to his workshop in the garage.

Later that morning, around 11:30, I told Mom that I didn't feel good and needed to lay down. I went into her bedroom and lay down on her bed. She came in and covered me with a blanket. I fell asleep.

I was laying on my back. When I woke up, around one o'clock, I felt my stomach was wet. I pulled back the blanket and saw that my nightgown was soaked. I lifted up my gown. Where the drain tube had been, my incision had burst open. I screamed for Mom. She came running into the room and saw what was happening. She went into the bathroom to grab a bath towel. She came back and told me to hold the towel on my stomach. She helped me get up and put on some slippers. She assisted me to the car.

Dad was sitting outside. Mom told him that my incision had burst open, and I needed to go to the hospital. Dad stayed home; he was afraid to see any family member in pain. When we got to the hospital, I was rushed into an emergency room. My blood pressure was 190 over 90. The bleeding had stopped, but I was in shock.

I explained to the doctor that I had had a hysterectomy on the fifth of July and gave him the name of the doctor and her phone number.

They did a blood test. After more than an hour, the doctor came back in. He had talked to Dr. Jenn. She said it was a simple infection in the incision, and they could take care of it. He told me that I needed surgery, but if there were any complications, I should go back to my doctor.

Mom and I left the hospital and went back home. We told Dad that I needed to go back to Detroit to see my own doctor. We packed our suitcases and left.

Mom had called my brother Hank, who lived in Mason. We would stay the night in Mason because Mom was concerned that the long drive was more than I could handle. It would be too late to call or see the doctor.

We arrived at Hank's around 7:30 that night. I was weak and needed help. Lou, my sister-in-law, and Mom helped me into the house and put me to bed. I passed out.

An hour or so later, I woke up. I was ringing wet from sweating. My hair and nightgown were soaking wet. I tried to move to throw the covers off. I was so weak that I couldn't move. I called for help. Mom and Lou came and helped me out of bed and out of my wet gown. They washed me up and put me in a clean gown. Mom said my fever must have broken. I went back to sleep.

We got up at six the next morning and left around 6:30. I was weak and chilled as we drove the rest of the way back to Detroit. We arrived back to my place around 8:30, and I called Dr. Jenn. I was told to come to her office immediately.

Mom helped me walk into the doctor's office. The doctor's assistant helped me into the examination room and onto the table.

When the doctor came into the room, her assistant and nurse

were with her. The nurse was at my head. The assistant was at my feet. Dr. Jenn put on a pair of gloves and picked up a scalpel. The nurse held me down by my arms, and the assistant held my legs. The doctor started to cut open my incision. The pain was excruciating. The nurse and assistant held me down so I couldn't move. She still kept cutting.

I screamed, "Can you give me something so I don't feel the pain? I can't take this." I was crying.

The doctor stopped. Her hands were shaking. She gave me a shot in my stomach. Several minutes later, she began to cut into me again.

I was terrified. "I still can feel the pain."

She replied, "I gave you a shot. You shouldn't feel anything."

I remembered something I learned a long time ago and snapped, "Infected tissue will not numb."

The nurse answered, "She's right, Doctor."

Dr. Jenn responded, "I need to cut the incision open." She went back to cutting. I couldn't stand the pain much more and almost passed out. Then she was done. I was crying.

The new incision was wide and deep. She washed, cleaned, and disinfected the incision, packing it with strip gauze. When I walked out into the waiting room, Mom was shocked. When she looked at me, she said, "Honey, you are as white as a sheet."

I could barely walk. I was glad when we got to my place. I lay down and fell asleep.

The next day, when I went back to the doctor's office, I was still facing more pain. Any healing that had taken place needed to be pulled out. Taking a pair of tweezers, the doctor removed any healing tissue. I gripped the table, shaking and crying.

It was Friday, and I was told I would need to clean and disinfect the incision myself over the weekend. I wasn't able to do it. I couldn't see down into the wound when I would lay down on my back and lift my head.

I called Carol. She came over to clean, disinfect, and pack the wound again. She taught Mom how to do it. Sunday, I went to the bathroom and left the door open.

Mom walked by the room and said, "Something smells terrible."

Within five days, I had two incisions burst open. The first incision was on my stomach, and the second burst inside me.

I called the doctor's emergency number. She called back in minutes. I explained to her what happened.

She said, "That's good. The incision inside you burst, allowing the infection to drain out. If it hadn't, you would have needed to go to the hospital."

For weeks, through the end of July, I had her pulling tissue out of my incision, five days a week. It was a painful ordeal.

I started feeling better. I was still tired but wanted to go home. I told the doctor. She wanted me to have an ultrasound test done first before she would agree to let me go. When Mom and I left to go for the ultrasound, we were already packed to go home.

The doctor who did the ultrasound test called Dr. Jenn and then gave me the phone.

After he was through talking to her, she said, "Ellen, you have a pocket of infection on your right side the size of a large grapefruit. There's another pocket of infection by your bladder, the size of a softball. I would prefer you stay here."

I answered, "I want to go home. I need to feel safe, secure, and peace of mind in order to heal."

She relented, saying, "I'll let you go home if you promise to rest. You get a fever or feel sick, I want you to get back here right away."

I said that I would. Mom and I were on our way home. I had two weeks before I needed to see Dr. Jenn again. I was still on antibiotics. Mom would need to clean and pack my incision every day.

When we arrived home, Dad was glad to see us. Being home was wonderful. After being home for about a week, Dad asked if I felt up to a boat ride, and I said yes.

The day was beautiful, with the sun shining, the river calm, with just a light breeze.

Dad drove slowly, going into the back waters. I saw a whistling swan for the first and only time. This native swan was being driven out by the mute swan. And Old World species introduced into North America, the mute swan is much larger and more aggressive. I felt renewed with nature all around me.

The two weeks went by fast. Mom and I headed back to Detroit. When I saw the doctor again, she pulled scabs and tissue out of my incision again to keep the wound open and infection draining. I wondered when this nightmare was going to end.

By the first of September, Mom needed to go home. I had healed enough. I was seeing the doctor once a week. The incision was still about half an inch deep. I could clean it myself.

I thanked her for taking care of me and being there. Telling her how much I loved her, I hugged and kissed her. Then she left.

I was crying after Mom was gone. I was lonely.

Ida saw me crying and told George, "Ellen's homesick; she'll move back home."

I wasn't able to drive. Carol would take me to the doctor for my appointments. Ida would go with me grocery shopping since I wasn't able to carry anything heavy.

I received a bill from the hospital in western Michigan and noticed a charge for a blood test. I realized that I hadn't received the results of the test. I called the hospital, wanting to know what the test findings were. The lady said I had a staph infection. I was scared because I knew that a staph infection could be fatal.

In mid-October, I had my last examination with Dr. Jenn. I had learned she loved chocolate. I had a prize-winning chocolate fudge cake recipe that I had gotten out of the newspaper years ago. I made one and brought it to her on my last appointment.

Dr. Jenn entered the examination room, and I gave her the cake. She cut a piece, picked it up with her fingers, and ate the cake, licking her fingers clean. She said she loved it.

She then put on a pair of gloves, without washing her hands, and proceeded to examine me, having her fingers inside of me.

I was shocked and said, "You didn't wash your hands."

She answered, "I put on gloves."

Before I could say anything else, she said I was fine and added that I could resume driving and go back to work. She left the room.

I thought back to every time I saw her, and never once did I see her wash her hands before examining me, even when she cut me open in the office. I wondered if she washed her hands before the surgery in the hospital.

In surgery, a glove can be nicked by a scalpel. If doctors or nurses don't wash their hands properly before the surgery, bacteria from their hand can infect the patient. Did this happen? I'll never know. Staph infections occur in hospitals. My infection was internal; that is why both incisions burst open.

I lost ten pounds and now weighed 109 pounds.

A few days after being back to work, I got a call from Dr. Jenn's office. The assistant said Dr. Jenn would love to have the recipe for the cake. I wouldn't owe her the balance of my bill if I gave her the recipe. I gave it to her and saved over four hundred dollars.

I was under the impression that the doctor was trying to buy my silence. What the doctor didn't know was that I wouldn't sue someone for making a mistake. I have made many mistakes myself. I believe that I need to accept being wrong and work toward a solution to correct what I did. I prayed that she would do the same. I was relieved that I wouldn't owe her any more money.

Jim had come to see me several times while I was recovering. He always looked concerned. In late October, I met him for coffee. He told me he was relieved to see me looking better. He had been worried when he first came to see me. He suspected that there was something more serious than an incision infection.

I told him everything: my stomach incision bursting, how the doctors at the other hospital advised me to go back to my doctor who did the surgery, the surgery I endured in Dr. Jenn's office, my internal incision bursting open, the results of the ultrasound, and learning from the blood test that I had a staph infection.

He said, "You should have been in the hospital. It's a miracle that you are even alive."

I told him that God had been with me. I know he saved my life and helped me through this whole horrible and painful ordeal.

He nodded and said, "You are a miracle."

Chapter 12
Mom and Dad's Health Change

After I went back to work, I realized how weak I still was. I'd come home from work exhausted. I'd lay down, fall asleep, and wake up the next morning. I would sleep ten to twelve hours a night. It took almost two years for me to get my strength back.

By November, I decided I wanted to move back home to western Michigan. Mom was in the hospital with pneumonia, and I wanted to be there with her. I had only been back to work for a month, so I knew that it was out of the question to go home. The normal recovery time for my surgery was six weeks, and I had already been gone for three and a half months. Mom was okay and had come home.

In March of 1986, I moved back to western Michigan, close to where I had lived before. It was comforting to be near my family once again.

In April of 1987, I moved even closer to Mom and Dad. I was concerned about them. They were getting up in years, and they needed help maintaining the house.

In 1990, I moved one block away from Mom and Dad. My apartment was beside a river and on the second floor, which turned out to be a blessing.

One morning in January 1993, I was on the phone with my

boss. I was working for another consulting firm, specializing in international quality standards.

I heard a loud noise and said, "Hold on, something is happening outside."

I put the phone down and went to the sliding glass doors. I looked out at the river and saw a huge piece of ice, fifty feet high, shooting straight up in the air. It was higher than the two-story building that my apartment was in. Then it came crashing down. It sounded like a bomb went off. The water came rushing over the bank.

I picked up the phone and told my boss that I was in a flood and needed to get out. I hung up the phone and called Mom. I told her what I had just seen and said I needed to get out of my apartment, and they probably should get out of their house too. I told her to meet me at the corner, on higher ground.

I ran downstairs to get the neighbor and her children. We got in her car and drove through the water on our road; we needed to get to the adjacent road, which was still dry.

Mom was waiting for us at the corner. I took her back to her house and we put her things up higher. We pulled the dresser drawers out and placed them on top of the beds. We piled items on countertops and tables. We had about an hour and a half before we needed to evacuate her house too. We did what we could, and then we left and checked into a hotel. Mom and Dad's road was much higher than the road that I lived on.

Mom had called Dad and told him to meet us at the hotel. We rented a room with two queen size beds, and we stayed there for eleven days.

When we were able to get back into our neighborhood, my apartment was fine. Mom and Dad's house was flooded. They stayed with me. During the week, Mom would go to their house to begin cleaning it up. I still needed to go to my job. On weekends, Mom and I would work on getting the house livable again.

Two nonprofit organizations came and gave Mom and Dad

vouchers to buy new mattresses, box springs, a bed, and a dresser. FEMA helped replace all of the appliances and furniture.

After almost six weeks, their house was back to livable conditions, and they went home.

In the spring, Dad went into the hospital with congestive heart failure. We learned that he needed open heart surgery. When the doctors opened him up, they found a benign tumor in his heart, the size of a golf ball. He was in the intensive care unit for fifty-seven days. He spent two additional weeks in the hospital and then two more weeks in rehabilitation.

By 1994, I was tired. I realized I had spent almost my entire adult life working sixty to sixty-five hours per week, sometimes more. This left little time to enjoy my life. I wanted a job that I could leave at the end of the day and not take my work home with me.

I mentioned this to Don, a client. He was the plant manager of a factory. He told me that he would be hiring in January and said that I should apply in December if I wanted the job. I did and got hired.

I started working the first of January as an assembler. My shift started at 5:55 a.m., and I worked until 2:25 p.m. each day. I had weekends off. I was relieved that I had time to enjoy life once again. I made less money, but I made enough to pay my bills and eat well. I was happy with my life again.

After work, I would go to Mom and Dad's house; I helped with repairs around the house. I would cut the grass and trim the yard in the summer and shovel snow from the walkway and driveway in the winter.

In March of 1998, I took Mom to the hospital. We returned once again in June. She was having trouble with breathing and felt heavy pressure on her chest. Both times, she received a breathing treatment and then was sent home. No tests were done either time.

The first week of September, I took Mom back to the hospital for a third time with the same symptoms. This time, they did order some tests.

When the doctor came into the room, he told Mom that she

had had a heart attack. She was going to be admitted immediately to the intensive care unit. Later, the doctors reassured me that she was doing fine and resting. They said that I could go home and come back to see her the following day.

I called Dad and reassured him that she was in good hands and resting. I called all my brothers and sisters, letting them know that Mom had had a heart attack, but she was stable. I explained that she was resting in ICU and added that they could all see her tomorrow.

The day before Mom came home, my sister Shelly, my niece, and I were with Mom when her personal physician, Dr. Giles, came in. He started telling Mom about her condition and the medications she would be on. He said that she would also have to follow up with a cardiologist.

Dr. Giles is a wonderful doctor. He is very caring and concerned for his patients. I sensed that something was missing from his conversation with Mom. I told Mom that I'd pick her up the next morning and followed him out of her room.

I approached Dr. Giles in the hallway and asked him about Mom's diagnosis. He explained that a virus had attacked Mom's heart, and the only real option would be a heart transplant. He also told me that Mom was too old for this operation. He said that she would only live three to five years with her heart, and most likely, closer to three years. He apologized and said, "I am sorry; I know this is difficult to hear."

He walked away; he hadn't told Mom his prognosis.

I stood there in shock. Tears began running down my face. I realized that my time with Mom was limited.

I went home to Mom and Dad's house. I was staying there to take care of Dad. I told Dad what Dr. Giles had said about Mom's heart and explained that it would become weaker and weaker over time. I shared that the doctor had told me that she would live maybe three years with medication. Dad just sat there with a look of fear and disbelief.

Later that evening, the phone rang, and I answered it. It was

Dr. Giles. He asked me if I had told anyone about Mom's limited time. I responded that I had told Dad but wasn't sure that he had understood.

Dr. Giles said to me, "Ellen, I don't want you to tell anyone else, especially your mom. I want her to enjoy her life. I am concerned that she would live in fear if she knew."

I promised that I wouldn't tell anyone else and hung up the phone.

I went into Mom's bedroom and lay down on her bed. I began crying, realizing that I would have to carry this painful burden myself. After a while, I stopped crying, After all, I still had Mom. I was going to enjoy all the time we had left together on this earth. *Doctors can be wrong,* I told myself. I wasn't going to let this prognosis dictate the future.

I knew Dad hadn't heard me crying. He didn't have his hearing aids in, and the TV was turned up too loud. I was thankful that he couldn't hear me crying.

I brought Mom home from the hospital the next day, and our life went on as usual.

Mom had been home for a little over a week. One day, I was at their house after work. Mom and Dad were in the living room, watching television. I was making dinner in the kitchen. Dad got up to go to the bathroom.

As he passed me on his way, he lost his balance. He said, "I'm okay," and went into the bathroom.

A few minutes later, he came out and stumbled again. I caught him before he fell.

He said, "Help me to my bed."

As I helped him lay down, I noticed the corner of his mouth was drooping.

He cried out, "My head," grabbing his head on the left side. He was in extreme pain.

I called out to Mom, "Call 911. Dad is having a stroke." I knew the signs, as I was a first medical response person at the factory where I worked.

Dad was taken to the hospital. We were told that he had indeed experienced a stroke.

The next day, Mom and all of us kids were there when the doctor came into Dad's room. He told us that Dad had had a massive stroke and would need to go to a nursing home for rehabilitation.

Dad ended up staying at the nursing home permanently because he refused to do the rehabilitation work. He could be stubborn sometimes. He was paralyzed on his right side and could no longer walk. He needed twenty-four-hour care, and Mom and I were not able to provide it at home.

In 1999, my landlord raised my rent $125 per month; he wanted the property to be more profitable, but I couldn't afford this increase. I was staying more and more at Mom and Dad's house. I told Mom about the increase in my rent and asked if I could move in with her. Mom was okay with me moving in, but she wanted to ask Dad for his approval. Dad said yes. He didn't want Mom to live alone. This arrangement was a win-win for both Mom and me.

Chapter 13
Mom Passing; Her Room and Smell

In March, Mom, Shelly, and my niece Maria were helping me pack and move. I was putting my furniture and belongings into storage. A few days later, Shelly stopped at Mom's after seeing Dad. She asked me if I would like a dog she had found. I really wanted the dog. Mom agreed, and I was thrilled.

Shelly told us how she found the dog. She had almost been hit by a car. Shelly stopped her car and called, "Here, Honey." and the dog came to her. There was a house across the street, so Shelly went there to see if the dog belonged to them. The woman said no. She told Shelly that the dog had been dumped off by a truck going down the road. It slowed down but didn't even stop as it threw the dog out of the moving truck. The lady at the house said that she didn't want the dog.

That very night, Shelly brought Honey (that was her name now) to our house. Honey was beautiful. She looked like a cocker spaniel and golden retriever mix. She was short, like a cocker, with long ears. Her face was like that of a golden retriever. Her hair was silky and the color of copper. The feathers on her legs and butt were blonde. Honey was extremely underweight. I told Shelly that I was concerned, believing the pup was sick.

I was so worried, I had Honey sleep with me. She felt very hot.

The next morning, I called Mom on my break from work and asked her how Honey was doing. Mom said that she was still laying on my bed and that she was hot to the touch. Mom had been putting cold compresses on her head and staying with her.

I asked Mom to call Shelly and to have her get an appointment with the vet. "Right after I got out of work," I told her.

Mom and I rushed Honey to the vet at 3:30 that afternoon. She was so sick. Her temperature was 105 °F. A dog's normal temperature is 102°F. She had internal parasites and was put on medication to kill the parasites as well as antibiotics to fight the infection that they were causing. The vet said Honey was around eight or nine months old, so still a puppy.

Honey was so afraid that I was going to kick her out that when I would take her out to go to the bathroom, she would cry and pull away from me on her leash. I would persuade her to come out with a piece of cheese and praise her when she came. I also needed to persuade her to come back inside the house with a piece of cheese. She was terrified of being thrown out and left alone.

Within several days, Honey realized that she was safe and knew that we were going to take care of her and love her. She had found her forever home.

Two months after moving in with Mom, I received my income tax return. I went to a furniture store looking for a sofa and chair for Mom. As long as I could remember, Mom had always had second-hand furniture. I wanted to surprise her with some new things. Even after the flood of 1993, Dad had purchased a used sofa. I was excited to give Mom this special surprise.

Dr. Giles wanted Mom to lose weight because it would help if her heart did not have to work as hard. Mom always listened to her doctor's advice. She quickly lost the weight he wanted her to. However, walking long distances was still difficult for her.

I came home from work one day and said, "Come on, Mom; we are going for a ride. It's a surprise."

I drove her to the furniture store and she got into the wheelchair.

I asked her to cover her eyes, and I pushed her through the store. In front of the sofa and matching chair that I had purchased for her, I said, "You can uncover your eyes, Mom. This is your new sofa and chair. I bought it for you."

Mom said, "Honey, is this for me?"

I answered, "Yes."

She replied, "It's beautiful. Thank you."

She had the biggest smile, and tears were welling up in her eyes. I was so glad to see her so happy. She certainly deserved it. Mom always put us kids first and herself last.

Mom wouldn't charge me rent. She wanted me to save my money for the future. I had more fun spending it on her. I would help her with buying groceries and other things that we needed at the house.

She had had very few vacations in her lifetime, because money was always tight with such a big family. Hank and Lou had taken Mom to an amusement park in Florida over twenty years ago. She still talked about how much she loved it, how much fun she had had. That trip meant a lot to her. I wanted to give her a vacation too, something special, just like Hank and Lou had given her years ago.

I started saving my money, and in December 1999, I put a down payment on a trip for the two of us to Tahiti. It was going to be an all-inclusive vacation for two weeks.

I was working overtime at the factory. This was extra money that I could save that I wouldn't have been able to without Mom's help not charging me rent. By March of 2000, I had the trip paid for in full.

In April, before our vacation, Mom and I went to a department store. She was looking for a new bedspread. She found one that cost $128.

Mom looked at me and said, "You can buy me the bedspread for Mother's Day."

I said okay and paid for it.

We walked past the jewelry counter, and I spotted a pair of

earrings that I wanted. While I was looking at the earrings, Mom tried on a fifteen carat London blue topaz ring. The gem was huge. Mom loved big gem rings.

Looking at her hand with the ring on, she said, "You can buy me this ring for Mother's Day."

I chuckled and answered, "I thought I just brought you the bedspread for Mother's Day."

She looked disappointed and answered, "Oh, I forgot."

I went back to the store later, bought the ring, and gave it to her on Mother's Day, and she was thrilled.

We landed in Tahiti the last week in June and stayed through the first week in July. We landed in the capital city of Tahiti, Pape'ete, and then flew to the island of Moorea. My luggage was damaged, so I needed to fill out a report. We took a later flight and then a taxi to the village where we would be staying.

When we came around a bend in the road, there was a beautiful blue lagoon with mountains in the background. Mom started to cry. I was afraid that she didn't like being here and said, "Mom, I am sorry."

She answered, "Oh, honey, it is so beautiful. More beautiful than I could have imagined."

The private village was gorgeous. There were bridges going over water with koi swimming in the ponds. There were gentle waterfalls and palm trees and flowers growing everywhere.

We had our own private bungalow with a deck.

The ocean was beautiful, with the water a turquoise blue. The water was so clear, you were able to see the bottom of the sea, fifty to sixty feet down.

French Polynesians have a high regard for senior citizens. Mom was treated with such love and care. It was endearing to see her be treated with such high respect by the locals.

The greatest joy I had was watching Mom laughing and giggling, playing games on the beach with the other guests. She went snorkeling for the first time. It was pure joy watching her feed fish out of her hand in the ocean. She loved how beautiful the ocean and fish were. We went swimming with the dolphins. It was amazing.

The host of the village had an awards assembly for guests who won the games. Awards were given out for all kinds of accomplishments, including participating for the first time in a new sport. Mom was called up on stage and won the award for being the oldest first-time snorkeler (she was eighty years old at the time). She was so excited. I was thrilled for her. I loved the attention that she was getting.

I wanted to get Mom a Tahitian black pearl. This is the only place in the world where they come from. I purchased one for each of us. Mom was humbled. She knew how expensive they were. I was so happy that I could give her a special keepsake that I knew she would cherish.

While we were in Tahiti, Shelly took care of Honey. She and Maria watered the flowers and cut the grass at the house too. We really appreciated their help.

Although the trip was wonderful, we were glad to go home. Honey was happy to see both of us. Mom often remarked on how I would give Honey a lot of attention. I would talk to her in baby talk and hug her. She would say, "I like dogs, but I don't gush over them like you do."

When I would come home from work, Mom would say with excitement, "Look what I taught Honey today."

There was always a new trick. I would chuckle and think to myself, *Yeah, Mom, you don't love her or give her attention.*

Honey would sleep with me on my bed. She loved Mom as much as me. Every morning, when I would leave for work, Honey would go into Mom's bedroom and lay down on the floor next to her bed. It was like she wanted to take care of her and protect her. She was a great watchdog.

After Dad went into the nursing home, Mom would go and see him almost every day. We would go together to visit him on the weekends.

Dad hated the food at the nursing home. They served a lot of frozen, processed food. On the weekends, Mom and I would bring him breakfast or dinner in insulated carriers to keep the food hot. Dad loved breakfast. I would make him an omelet with ham or sausage, cheese, and green peppers. He was in seventh heaven.

In late August 2001, my uncle, Mom's brother, was showing me pictures of his wedding in 1950. There was a picture of Mom and Dad. They looked so young. Mom was in a beautiful dress, Dad in a suit. Dad hated getting dressed up. I don't remember ever seeing him in a suit. They both looked wonderful.

There were some objects in the foreground and background that were detracting from this lovely picture of my parents. I asked my uncle if I could borrow the picture, and he agreed. I wanted to take it to a professional photographer to have the objects removed. Their anniversary was coming up in October. It would be sixty-two years that they were married. I wanted to give them the finished photo for their special day.

The picture turned out spectacular. I had six copies made, one for Mom and Dad, and five for each of us kids. I was going to give each brother and sister one for Christmas.

Mom and I went to see Dad on their anniversary. I gave them the picture. Mom loved it. Dad said, "I was a handsome dude." I laughed and assured him that yes, he was. That turned out to be a special gift; it was their last anniversary together.

Mom and I had grown closer than ever. I had shared with her my experience with the devil. In November, Mom asked me how I was able to get rid of him. I told her that I had asked God for his help. He protected me and got rid of Satan. A few days later, Mom told me that she prayed, asking God to protect her from Satan and take care of her. She confided that God answered her prayers as well.

Mom's birthday was December 3. Early that morning, she asked me to come to bed with her. As I lay there, she hugged me, told me that I was a special daughter, and said how grateful she was to have me. She told me how much she loved me, saying it wasn't going to be long before she would be leaving to be with God. I was crying, hugging, and kissing her.

I told her, "I don't want you to die. If you die, I want to die too."

She tried to reassure me and said, "Honey, you're going to be okay. You are a strong young woman."

All I could say was, "No, I don't want you to die."

She said, "I know you'll be okay. I love you, Ellen. You are a good daughter."

We lay there for a while, hugging each other in silence.

December 15 was our last day together. Around two o'clock in the morning, the nursing home called, telling us Dad had been sent to the hospital. Mom and I got dressed and went to meet him at the hospital. When we arrived, we were told that Dad was fine and he had already been sent back to the nursing home. I asked Mom if she wanted to go see him, and she said, "No, we'll see him later today," so we went home.

When we got home, neither of us was tired. We were wide awake, so Mom said, "Let's have some cocoa and hot buttered toast." This was one of our favorite treats. It tasted so good.

Later in the day, we went shopping for Christmas, buying presents and food for when the family would be coming for the holiday. On our way home, Mom wanted to go see Dad. He was happy to see us. Mom and Dad were very loving to each other, hugging and kissing. When we were getting ready to leave, Mom said to Dad, "I love you. I'll see you tomorrow."

Dad replied, "I love you too," and they kissed each other goodbye.

When we got home, I told Mom, "Honey, you look tired. Go inside and rest. I'll carry everything into the house."

On my third trip, Mom was at the side door, letting out a horrible sound and gasping for air. I dropped everything and ran to her.

"Mama, what's wrong?" I asked.

She couldn't speak. She patted her upper back.

I said, "Do you have something stuck in your throat?"

She nodded yes.

I said, "Let me do the Heimlich maneuver," as I moved behind her and put my arms around her torso.

I tried twelve to fifteen times, but I couldn't get whatever it was dislodged. "Mama, I need help," I told her. I took her by the hand and helped her to a chair next to the phone and sat her down.

I called 911 and said, "I need help. My mother has something stuck in her throat and can't breathe. She's eighty-two years old."

They knew the address with caller ID. The 911 operator said, "Help is on the way." So I hung up the phone and turned my concern back to Mom.

Her head was hanging down. I said, "Mama, hang in there; they're coming."

She lifted her head up, looking at me. Her eyes were filled with tears and sadness, as if to say, "I'm sorry."

Her eyes rolled back in her head, and she collapsed in my arms. I heard her breath leaving her body. I laid her down on the floor, terrified. I told her, "Mama, they're coming. Please don't leave me. Please don't die."

Trembling, I didn't know what I could do with her having something stuck in her throat.

Within minutes, the ambulance was there. The emergency medical technicians started working on her. I called all my brothers and sisters to tell them that Mama had collapsed. The EMTs continued working on her.

I went outside. I couldn't bear to watch them working on Mom. I was trembling and shaking so hard, I couldn't even hold a cigarette.

After about fifteen minutes, one of the EMTs came to me to tell me that Mom was gone. She said that she was so sorry for my loss. She explained that Mom didn't have anything stuck in her throat, but that she had had a heart attack. Her heart was beating slower and slower when she wasn't able to breathe. This gave her a feeling like she had something stuck in her throat. Her heart just stopped.

The EMT helped me back inside, and I sat in a chair by Mom.

Honey came over and lay down beside her. She was crying out loud and licking Mom's hand. The EMT tried shooing Honey away.

I said, "You leave her alone. She loves Mom. She needs to grieve too."

Honey lay next to Mom, crying for some time, and then she came over to me. I hugged her. I knew she was hurting, just like I was.

The next morning, all of us kids went to tell Dad what had happened. He sat there in disbelief. I could see fear and pain in his eyes with his sad expression.

The funeral and the days that followed were a blur for me. Even Christmas was not the happy occasion we were used to. This was the last Christmas we all had together as a family. Mom was the glue that held our family together.

I closed Mom's bedroom door right after she passed away. I couldn't bear the pain of looking in, much less going into her room.

From the time of Mom's passing until I went back to work, there were always others in the house.

Surprisingly, Honey never tried to get into Mom's room. The door to her bedroom was difficult to close. The house had settled over the years, and in order to close the door, I needed to turn the door knob while lifting the door at the same time. Then I could pull the door shut. I had to line up the door latch before I could successfully shut the door; it was also difficult to open. The latch was stuck in the hole in the door jam. The door knob was then hard to turn.

My first day back to work was several weeks after Mom's passing. When I came home, the door to Mom's bedroom was open, and Honey was lying next to Mom's bed, as she had done while Mom was alive.

Mom had a set of stainless-steel mixing bowls that were too big to fit in a cabinet. There were four bowls altogether, and the smaller bowls nested in the largest bowl, which was twenty-four inches across. Mom stored these bowls under her bed because they were so big.

Strangely, the bowls were now out in the middle of the room, lined up in order, from the largest to the smallest. I was confused how this could have happened.

I questioned how Honey could have opened the door, since I had a difficult time getting it opened once it was shut tight. I looked at the door. There were no scratches or claw marks. I thought maybe she just got lucky opening the door but didn't really know how she could have done this.

Honey could have pushed the bowls out into the middle of the room, but lining them up in graduated size and order? I couldn't come up with a good explanation for this at all.

Every night when I would come home from work, I would find Honey in Mom's room, lying next to Mom's bed. The mixing bowls would be in the middle of the room, lined up in order. This went on for about eight to ten days, always on the days that I worked, never on weekends. Maybe Honey had gotten lucky once, but not ten times.

The tenth day when I came home from work, the bedroom door was once again open, and Honey was lying next to Mom's bed. The bowls were lined up again in the middle of the room. I went into the living room. Behind the sofa, one of the blinds was opened. I always kept the blinds shut to keep the sun from fading the furniture. In order to open the blind, there is a long rod that needs to be twisted. There is no way a dog could turn that rod.

Mom had trained Honey to stay off the sofa. She was not allowed on any furniture, except for my bed. I tried to get Honey to lay with me on the sofa many times after Mom died. She just wouldn't do it. Even if I picked her up and held her in my arms, she would fight, wiggle, and squirm to get down. She wouldn't have anything to do with being on the sofa. Even if she did get onto the sofa, I still couldn't figure out how she could have opened the blind.

We had a gas space heater in the living room. There was a wood table and chair a couple feet from the space heater. Mom would sit at the table and play solitaire. I had passed that chair where she sat many times to turn the heat up or down. That same day that the blind was open, I went to turn the heat up. As I did, I passed the chair Mom sat in and I smelled her scent. Every person has their own scent. It was as if she was sitting right there. Wood doesn't absorb a person's scent.

After the tenth day, Mom's bedroom door stayed closed. Honey was always lying on my bed when I came home from work.

I have never been able to come up with a logical answer for the strange events that happened.

Mom lived three years, two and a half months after her diagnosis by Dr. Giles.

Chapter 14
Praying for Dad; Vision

After Mom passed away, I struggled with losing her. I was scared of the pain I would go through. I felt alone and isolated. I knew all my brothers and sisters were hurting, just as much as I was.

There were times I felt I had nothing to live for. I would go to work every day and do my job, pretending everything was fine. I was an emotional wreck.

If I had an experience during the day, I would think, *I need to tell Mom.* Then I'd realize she was gone. Coming home from work, I would drive around the corner and see Mom's car in the driveway and think, *Oh, Mom is home.* I was excited for a second. Then reality set in. I felt empty and alone, knowing she was gone.

Mom was more than my mother. She was my best friend. I missed her. I had an emptiness inside that no one else could fill. I was so grateful I had Honey to come home to, giving me affection that I needed.

At the same time, Dad was struggling with the loss of Mom. I was concerned what would happen. They were married sixty-two years, a lifetime together.

I often got a call from the nursing home in the middle of the night. I would be told Dad was yelling, screaming, and thrashing about. They were worried he would fall out of bed and hurt himself.

He was keeping his roommate and other patients awake. Would I please come help calm him down? I told them I would.

When I arrived, Dad had been put in a waiting room, away from the other patients, with the nurse being able to watch him. A full-size mattress was on the floor so Dad would be safe from falling. He lay there, yelling and swearing. I lay down beside him, talking to him in a calm voice.

"Daddy, I am here. I get scared too. It's okay."

I would gently stroke the top of his head, letting him know I loved him. I talked to him for a couple of hours, until he calmed down and fell asleep.

I would get a call from the nursing home for me to come and help calm Dad down at least once a week.

I would go and see Dad after work two or three times during the week.

On weekends, I would make him breakfast, of course, an omelet, his favorite, and fresh fruit on the side.

In February, before my birthday, I broke down. I went into Mom's room. I lay down on her bed, hugging and smelling her pillow. I needed to feel close to her as I grieved losing her. I lay there crying and shaking all over for the longest time. Honey had come into the room, lying next to the bed, being with me and comforting me as I grieved. She gave me what I needed and helped me through the pain.

In April, Pastor Tom helped me bring my dad home for the day. His son was wheelchair bound, so his van was equipped with an electric chair lift, making it easier to bring Dad home. Pastor Tom pushed Dad in the wheelchair into the house and then left. I would call him when it was time to bring Dad back to the nursing home.

Dad had not attended Mom's funeral. I was concerned he hadn't totally understood that Mom was gone. I believed he needed closure. Mom had been cremated, and I still had her ashes at the house. I brought the container with Mom's ashes to Dad, explaining what they were. He placed the container on his lap. He looked extremely sad. I hugged him and left the room, allowing him to grieve and accept Mom's death. I understood how difficult this was for him.

After a while, Dad called me back into the room. He handed me the container and was silent.

I took Dad outside, down by the water. He was listening to the birds and watching the boats on the river. Being surrounded by nature seemed to lighten his mood. Dad loved being by the water. We had lunch outside, enjoying each other's company. Later in the day, Pastor Tom and I took Dad back to the nursing home.

In September, all of us kids and some of his grandchildren came to the nursing home to celebrate Dad's eighty-fifth birthday. I got two cakes, one chocolate and one white, since there was a matter of different tastes in the family. Dad's face lit up, smiling from ear to ear. It was wonderful seeing him having a good day.

From the time I moved one block from Mom and Dad, I began to understand Dad's fear he had with God accepting him. Dad was raised in a strict Christian home. He felt unworthy of God's love, especially after what he did in the war.

Dad felt a tremendous responsibility to fight and protect our country, yet killing went against his faith. He believed God would never forgive him, when it was Dad who couldn't forgive himself. I believe we need to ask for forgiveness, accept being wrong, and forgive ourselves, so we can forgive others.

When we were alone, I'd tell Dad our Lord is forgiving. All he needed to do is ask God to forgive him, and God would. Dad felt he wasn't worthy. He said many times that he would probably be going to Hades. I prayed every night for God to forgive and accept him.

After Dad's birthday, he started to slowly withdraw from reality. While I was with him, he would ask why Mom hadn't come to see him lately. I would remind him that Mom had passed away.

All of us kids tried to help Dad. Hank and Ann came on Thanksgiving, bringing a wonderful meal. He perked up then. All the kids came to see him periodically. My brothers and sisters were scattered like the four winds, living in different cities. With all of them working, it was difficult for all of them to come. I was only ten minutes from the nursing home.

There were times I felt guilty and ashamed. I didn't want to go see Dad. Watching him slowly deteriorate mentally and physically was more painful than I could bear sometimes. I still went during the week and on the weekends because I knew he needed his family, no matter how painful it was for me.

The first of the year 2003, Dad started to hallucinate while I was with him. He would tell me Mom was standing in the doorway and ask why she wouldn't come in. Other times, he would tell me Mom came to see him. He would get angry and want to know why Mom hadn't come to see him lately. Every time, I would tell him Mom was gone, she had passed away. He would look confused and disappointed. His answer was always, "Oh."

I was hurting and felt helpless. I knew we were losing him.

In late June, we were told Dad was slowly dying. He would only be with us a matter of weeks. He had lost a lot of weight and grown weak. Hospice was with him.

Knowing we were losing Dad, when I got home after visiting him, I would pray for him. One day, around four o'clock in the afternoon, I was sitting in Mom's chair that she sat in, watching television.

I sat there looking out into the room and prayed, "Dear Lord, it's not going to be too long, and Dad will be leaving us. Please forgive him. He is too ashamed to ask for forgiveness for himself. Please accept him."

Christ appeared before me. He was dressed in white, wearing brown sandals. His arms and hands were reaching out to me. I saw his loving, caring expression. His eyes were full of compassion. He spoke to me internally. "My dear Ellen, I am with him, and he is with me."

I sat there crying and thanking him. Then he was gone. I was so relieved, knowing Daddy was going to be with our Lord. I'll always remember his loving, caring eyes.

Chapter 15
Vision of Mom and Dad in Heaven

On the weekends, I would bring Dad breakfast. He was always happy to see me, although his appetite had decreased. Before, Dad would eat all of his breakfast. Now, he would eat about a third.

We sat in the cafeteria with other patients at the table. I was hoping for a private moment to tell Dad what Christ told me. It never happened. During the week, when I'd go to see him, he was always asleep. After seeing Dad, I cried a lot on my way home, watching him slowly giving up.

On July 6, at seven in the morning, the nursing home called to tell me that they couldn't wake Dad up. He was in a coma. They believed that he had a stroke.

I called Shelly and told her what was happening. All of us met at the nursing home. We sat with Dad all day long. The nurse would come every three hours, giving Dad morphine on a sponge. He would suck on it to ease his pain.

When people are in a coma, they can hear everything that is said. Their hearing is the last to go before death. We took turns sitting next to Dad, rubbing his head. When one of us took our hand away from touching and rubbing his head, he would move his head about, searching for our hand. Our touch gave him comfort.

We all told Dad how much we loved him. We all understood he

91

loved all of us. It was okay for him to leave us and be at peace and be together with Mom. We had learned two days before Dad went into a coma that he told his nurse that all he wanted to do was to be with his wife.

We asked the nurse how long before Dad would pass away.

She said, "It could be an hour, a day, a week. There is no way of knowing."

Later, each of us spent time alone with Dad. While I was with Dad, just the two of us, I told him Christ stood before me. I said, "Daddy, Christ told me he is with you. He told me that you would be with him. He loves you."

I know that Dad heard every word I said. He rubbed his head into my hand, with tears running down his face. I said, "Daddy, I love you, and He does too. I know he told me."

I was crying as I hugged and kissed him. I told him that he was going to be okay.

The hours dragged on. About one o'clock in the morning, Hank said, "Ellen, why don't you go home and get some sleep? We'll call you if anything changes."

I went home and lay down, trying to sleep. I lay there, knowing we were going to lose Dad. I didn't want to let him go. I also didn't want him to be in pain. I was crying. Honey was lying next to me. She was licking my hand, trying to comfort me. I couldn't sleep.

Around six in the morning, I went back to the nursing home. Nothing had changed. Each of us took turns sitting with Dad and comforting him. We had all been awake over twenty-four hours. My brothers and sisters were tired. They all wanted to go home and get some much-needed rest. I told them I would stay. If anything changed, I would call them right away.

Every three hours, the nurse would come and give Dad morphine for his pain.

Sometime in the middle of the afternoon, the nurse came in to give him his morphine. I asked her if there was any change. She said, "No; it could be hours or even days. There is no way of knowing."

About twenty minutes later, Dad started breathing heavily. I got scared and ran to the nurse's station. I told the nurse to call Shelly. Dad was getting worse. I went back to Dad's room. As I came into the room, he was sitting straight up in bed and then fell back down. I screamed in fear. The nurse came running in to check his vitals.

She turned to me, said, "I am sorry, he's gone," and then left the room.

I froze, realizing Dad was gone. Crying, I went over to him and kissed him goodbye, and left his room. I went outside, needing to be alone, and sat there, crying, for the longest time.

We had a visitation and a service at the funeral home. Pastor Tom gave the eulogy. Dad had been cremated. He always wanted a burial at sea. He had his captain's license his whole adult life. He was in charge of a ship during the war.

Mom and I made arrangements with the Coast Guard for Dad to be buried at sea in Lake Michigan; this was carried out, with all of us kids taken out on the ship.

Every night before I went to bed, I'd get down on my knees, beside my bed, look up, and pray, thanking God for all the wonderful gifts he has given me.

Two weeks after Dad's burial at sea, I was praying at night, thanking God for all of his blessings and asking him to take care of my family. Suddenly, my room lit up. I had a vision before me. Our Lord was sitting there, beams of light like the rays of the sun shooting out behind him. I could only see the outline of his head. He was dressed in a white robe, with a gold braided belt. He was wearing gold braided sandals. Mom was to his right, and Dad was to his left. Our Lord held both of them in his arms. Mom and Dad were young and healthy. Both were smiling, looking happy. I was overwhelmed, crying tears of joy.

I said, "Thank you, Lord." Then the vision was gone.

Sandy and I work together and became good friends over the years. She and her husband Burt and I attended church together. I shared some of my spiritual experiences with Sandy in the past.

The next day at work, I told Sandy about the vision I had. I couldn't understand why I couldn't see Christ's face. When he stood before me, I saw His face then.

She said, "Because it was our heavenly Father. We are not worthy to look at him. Only through Christ, with his forgiveness, will we be able to see him."

I realized that she was right. I also remembered the Bible says our bodies would be renewed, just like Mom's and Dad's were.

A few days later, I was talking to Pastor Tom. I had told him about some of my spiritual experiences, including the last one with my parents and our heavenly Father. I told him I was grateful yet humbled.

I said, "But why me? Sometimes, I am not a very good Christian. There was a time when I didn't believe at all. I am not famous or holy. I am just an average person."

Pastor Tom answered, "Why not you? Maybe it is because you didn't believe. For you to bear witness that He does exist. You need to tell your story."

I thought about it. I promised God I would write my story. That was in 2003. It was the last wonderful experience I had, or so I thought.

Chapter 16
The Brush with Death

I forgot about my promise to God and went on with my life. My next-door neighbor, Dave, liked to take Honey for walks every day. She just loved to go with him, especially since Dave would spoil her with all kinds of treats. Honey was getting fat.

I told him, "I know you love her, but please cut down on the treats."

Dave laughed and said, "Honey looks fine."

Alice, his wife, reminded him that Honey was my dog, and he needed to cut back on the treats.

Dave and Alice moved away before Mom died. Honey would go to their house every day, waiting for her friend, even after they were gone. Their house was vacant for years. A real estate company purchased it and remodeled it to sell.

One day, Honey went over to the house. The door was open, and she went in, looking for Dave. I followed her, knocked on the door, and walked in, telling the people that my dog had come into the house.

There was a man and two women. They said they were there to clean the house. One of the women asked me if Honey was my dog. I said yes and explained that she used to have a friend who lived here and would take her for walks. She was still looking for him, even after he moved away years ago. I apologized for interfering. I just came in to get my dog.

The same woman said, "I want your dog."

I was shocked and answered, "No, I love her. I would never give her up."

She blurted out, "Well, I want her."

I said, "No, not for all the money in the world."

She answered, "She's such a wonderful dog."

I took Honey and went home.

One of the men who was working on the house was friends with the woman who wanted Honey. Three weeks later, after the encounter with the woman, I came home from work, and Honey was gone. I could never prove they took her. To this day, I still miss her.

My sister Sara had a heart of gold. She always took care of others. There wasn't a birthday or a holiday she forgot. She always put others before herself.

Sara was diagnosed with a rare skin disease that attacks your internal organs. It's a disease that progresses slowly over the years. It also affects the immune system. Sara's disease attacked her heart and lungs.

Over the years, she progressively deteriorated. In the fall of 2010, Sara was on oxygen and had been in the hospital several times for pneumonia and congestive heart failure.

Sara was looking forward to the holidays. She was able to be home, having a hospital bed set up in her living room.

When I was talking to her on the phone, she mentioned she wished she could get the carpet cleaned in her living room before Thanksgiving. I told her I'd gladly come and clean her carpet, since I had a carpet shampooer.

I went to her house the Sunday before Thanksgiving. Sara had lost a lot of weight. She was on oxygen and bedridden but was still her old self, happy and caring, talking about the future, and looking forward to the upcoming holidays. Her daughters would be preparing Thanksgiving dinner, with her whole family coming.

After I cleaned the carpet, Sara and I talked about the past experiences we had together, laughing and giggling. We kissed and hugged each other, saying, "I love you. See you later."

In our family, we'd never say goodbye. Goodbye was final a word we would never say to each other.

Saturday morning after Thanksgiving, my niece called to tell me Sara died. Both of us were crying.

She said, "Dad asked Mom what she wanted for breakfast and to give her her medication. She told Dad she didn't need it right now. And Mom asked Dad to turn off the light. It was too bright. Dad told her the light was off. She answered, saying, 'Well, it sure is bright but okay.' She then closed her eyes to rest. Dad kissed her and went into the kitchen to make breakfast. When he went to bring Mom a cup of coffee, she had passed away."

I believe Dad saw the light; he was paralyzed and couldn't get up without help. When I walked into his room, he was sitting straight up in bed. He was looking straight up. Then he fell back in bed and was gone. The same as my sister Sara, seeing the light.

I have been so blessed to receive such precious gifts, to see my parents with my heavenly Father. I also believe my sister is with Mom and Dad in heaven.

I procrastinated over the years. I came up with all kinds of excuses, putting off writing my story: I wouldn't know how to write it. English was my weakest subject in school. I am not an author. I don't know any publishers. How would I come up with the money if it was published? Of course, I had the answers to all my excuses. I was scared to write it. How would I start?

On September 19, 2017, at 8:30 in the morning, I was on my way to work, heading south. A car was coming from the opposite direction, going north. I was doing the speed limit of 55 mph. The other car made a sudden left turn in front of me. I was thirty feet from the other car. I knew I was going to hit head-on with my car, yet I was calm; I felt safe. I should have been terrified.

I hit head-on with my car, hitting the right fender, just in front of the passenger door. My car spun around, slamming my left side of my car into the other car.

I was pushing the other car. The only thing that stopped my car from still moving was the stop sign that I slammed into.

Smoke was billowing out of the engine, filling the interior of the car. I could hardly breathe. I was afraid that the car was going to catch on fire. A man stopped and quickly disconnected my battery.

The steering wheel was only inches from my chest. I thought I was fine until I tried to get out on the passenger side. I had a sharp pain in my breast bone. The passenger door was jammed. A man and a woman helped pry the door open to help me out.

The emergency medical technician asked me how fast I was going. I told him that I was going 55 miles per hour. He looked shocked. I didn't know why.

At the hospital, I learned that I had a fractured sternum as well as a bloody nose.

The next day, the insurance adjuster called. He had the police report and had seen my car. He told me with the speed I was going and the distance of only thirty feet before impact, I should have been killed instantly. No seatbelt or airbag can protect a person at that speed hitting head-on. I was wearing my seatbelt.

A couple days later, I spoke to my insurance agent. He made the same statement as the adjuster. I should have been killed instantly. He was concerned about my injury and amazed I was alive.

Now I understood why the ambulance emergency medical technician looked shocked.

I then realized why I was calm and felt safe when I knew I was going to hit the other car. God had been with me, protecting me, as he had so many times in the past.

I remembered my promise I made to God that I would write my story. I know God exists. He sent me an angel to help me, even when I didn't believe. He protected me from Satan and sent me help when I was lost. He protected me from harm many times, saved my life several times, and answered my prayers beyond my expectations.

Yes, I know God exists. He has been with me many times, in my hour of need. I love Him with all my heart and soul.